The Arnold and Caroline Rose Monograph Series
of the American Sociological Association

Education, employment, and migration

Israel in comparative perspective

Other books in the series

J. Milton Yinger, Kiyoshi Ikeda, Frank Laycock, and Stephen J. Cutler: *Middle Start: An Experiment in the Educational Enrichment of Young Adolescents*

James A. Geschwender: *Class, Race, and Worker Insurgency: The League of Revolutionary Black Workers*

John Low-Beer: *Protest and Participation: The New Working Class in Italy*

Orrin E. Klapp: *Opening and Closing: Strategies of Information Adaptation in Society*

Rita James Simon: *Continuity and Change: A Study of Two Ethnic Communities in Israel*

Marshall B. Clinard: *Cities with Little Crime: The Case of Switzerland*

Volumes previously published by the American Sociological Association

Michael Schwartz and Sheldon Stryker: *Deviance, Selves and Others*

Robert M. Hauser: *Socioeconomic Background and Educational Performance*

Morris Rosenberg and Roberta G. Simmons: *Black and White Self-Esteem: The Urban School Child*

Chad Gordon: *Looking Ahead: Self-Conceptions: Race and Family as Determinants of Adolescent Orientation to Achievement*

Anthony M. Orum: *Black Students in Protest: A Study of the Origins of the Black Student Movement*

Ruth M. Gasson, Archibald O. Haller, and William H. Sewell: *Attitudes and Facilitation in the Attainment of Status*

Sheila R Klatzky: *Patterns of Contact with Relatives*

Herman Turk: *Interorganizational Activation in Urban Communities: Deductions from the Concept of System*

John DeLamater: *The Study of Political Commitment*

Alan C. Kerckhoff: *Ambition and Attainment: A Study of Four Samples of American Boys*

Scott McNall: *The Greek Peasant*

Lowell L. Hargens: *Patterns of Scientific Research: A Comparative Analysis of Research in Three Scientific Fields*

Charles Hirschman: *Ethnic Stratification in Peninsular Malaysia*

Education, employment, and migration

Israel in comparative perspective

Paul Ritterband
Associate Professor
City College and Graduate Center
City University of New York

Cambridge University Press

Cambridge
London   New York   Melbourne

Published by the Syndics of the Cambridge University Press
The Pitt Building, Trumpington Street, Cambridge CB2 1RP
Bentley House, 200 Euston Road, London NW1 2DB
32 East 57th Street, New York, NY 10022, USA
296 Beaconsfield Parade, Middle Park, Melbourne 3206, Australia

First published 1978

Printed in the United States of America
Typeset by Jay's Publishers Services, Inc., North Scituate, Mass.
Printed and bound by the Murray Printing Company, Westford, Mass.

Library of Congress Cataloging in Publication Data
Ritterband, Paul.
Education, employment, and migration.
(The Arnold and Caroline Rose monograph series
of the American Sociological Association)
Includes bibliographical references and index.
1. Israeli students in the United States.
2. Education, Higher – Israel. 3. Brain drain – Israel.
I. Title. II. Series: The Arnold and Caroline Rose
monograph series in sociology.
LB2376.3.I75R57   301.32'8   76–62584
ISBN 0 521 21586 2 hard covers
ISBN 0 521 29192 5 paperback

Chapter 2 is a revision of "The Determinants of Motives of Israeli
Students Studying in the United States," *Sociology of Education*,
volume 42, number 4, Fall 1969.

An earlier version of a part of Chapter 4 was published as
"Law, Policy and Behavior," *American Journal of Sociology*,
volume 76, number 1, July 1970.

For my parents
Joseph and Augusta Ritterband

Contents

Preface

In the 1960s the term *brain drain* came into popular usage to describe the international migration of high-level manpower. The brain-drain issue was discussed in national legislatures, United Nations agencies, and made the headlines in newspapers around the world. Much or most of the discussion took place in a political context in which "blame" for the brain drain was assessed and placed upon the shoulders of those nations benefiting from this migration. Little attention was given to the determinants of the brain drain aside from the simplistic assertion that the rich nations were exploiting the poor in a new form of economic colonialism. *Education, Employment, and Migration* is a study of one particularly vexing form of brain drain, the permanent migration of overseas students.

A significant portion of the brain drain to the United States comes about when foreign students decide to remain in the United States after completing their studies. In most instances, they initially arrive in the United States as students, subsequently changing their legal status to that of immigrant, and ultimately remain in the United States. *Education, Employment, and Migration* focuses on the student's educational experience in his home country as a determinant of his studying in the United States and shows how that educational experience is linked to his career opportunities in his home country's labor market.

The study first engages in a detailed analysis of the experience of Israeli students in the United States. It begins with an account of the ways in which the Israeli educational system allocates opportunity *within* the schools all the way up to graduate study. It shows how relative success or failure in the Israeli schools determines both the student's reasons for study abroad and the point at which he will study abroad. The study then goes on to examine the relationship between Israel's educational system and occupational opportunity structure, showing how this relationship in turn is a key determinant of the migration decision. The impact of educational success on occupational opportunity

ix

and ultimately on the migration decision is shown to vary significantly by sector of the economy. These relationships reflect characteristics of Israeli social structure and history. The study proceeds to examine national brain-drain policies, both operational and projected, and develops a method for determining the utility of alternative policies.

The Israeli experience is generalized through the analysis of two multinational data sets. The major Israeli findings are replicated among other national groups studying in the United States, whereas some important variations from the American patterns are shown among foreign students resident in France. In the course of this analysis, national rates of brain drain are computed and accounted for. The last section of the book looks at the costs and benefits of study abroad for the sending and receiving countries. It looks to the home country's level of development to explain the student's educational success in the United States and, ultimately, his professional achievement.

I would like to acknowledge debts I have incurred in the course of the work leading to this book.

First, my thanks and appreciation to my wife Ruth, who endured my obsessive mumblings and groanings over computer output, theoretical missteps, and general analytic angst.

I am grateful to Herbert H. Hyman and Robert K. Merton for their lectures, writings, and conversation.

To Yigal Allon (then Minister of Labor and now Deputy Prime Minister) and Avraham Ben Zvi (then Director of the Israel Government Bureau for Professionals), both of the State of Israel, my thanks for bringing their policy problem to me and encouraging me materially and morally in the analysis of the problem and the search for solutions. My understanding of the logic and method of reason analysis owes much to the tutelage of Charles G. Kadushin. The conceptual and editorial skill of Ida Harper Simpson, her editorial board, and the anonymous referees turned drafts into finished copy.

Steven M. Cohen, Evelyn Geller, and Harold S. Wechsler generously gave their time to read all or parts of the manuscript. Joseph Lopatin and Peter Abrams of the Calculogic Corporation supplied efficient and precise data processing skills. Naomi Even Rubenstein served as a responsible research assistant during the early part of the project. Muriel Bennett typed innumerable drafts with speed, patience, and accuracy.

The Israeli data collection and early analysis were supported by grants from the United States Office of Education and the Ministry of

Labor of the State of Israel. The cross-national work was supported by a grant from the Ford Foundation. The costs of typing were defrayed by a grant from the Meinhard Spielman Fund of the Department of Jewish Studies of the City College of the City University of New York. Clara Shapiro deftly managed the grant funds and helped keep the project solvent. The data for the cross-national analyses were kindly made available by William Glaser and Seymour Warkov.

To all who helped and encouraged me, both known and unknown, my thanks and appreciation.

New York   P.R.
March, 1977

1. Introduction: the dimensions of the problem

On the 17th of June in the year 1621, Czar Michael of Russia wrote to King James I of England, saying:

> Whereas about 18 years past, in the time of the Emperor and greate Duke Burris Pheodorowich of all Russia there was wnt into your Majesties Dominiones fower young gentlemen of our Kingdome . . . to trayned upp in the English and Lattin tongs and soe to be retorned againe and delivered to the Lordes of our Counsell . . . [and these young men had been] deteyned and kept in England against their wills.[1]

Evidently Czar Michael was not satisfied with the action taken by King James to repatriate the Russian "exchange students," for on January 4th, 1622, the Russian ambassador to England underscored the czar's request with a petition to the Privy Council, attributing the apparent reluctance of Russian students to return to external factors – the "long troubles in our Country of Russia."[2]

These efforts were futile. Of the original four students, two had since died, one was resident in Ireland, and the fourth, though agreeing to meet with the Russian ambassador, refused repatriation. The matter then came to the attention of Sir John Merrick, the English ambassador to Russia, who expressed sympathy for the migrant. Writing the Privy Council, Merrick indicated that he felt all that might properly be done had been done, and he now "humbly besought the Kinges Majeste that he [the Russian student] might not (against the law of Nationes) be forced out of the land."[3]

In the years since that correspondence, the numbers of students engaged in what is now called international educational exchange and the problem of student nonreturn have both grown enormously. Among the states of the Atlantic community alone the number of foreign students enrolled reached almost a quarter million by 1965.[4] Their problems, no longer handled in the discreet diplomatic correspondence that characterized an earlier time, are widely discussed in international conferences and legislatures, and are reported in the daily press. Yet,

1

despite the change in volume of educational exchange and in the form and forum of discussion, the basic issues remain those raised in the Anglo-Russian correspondence: the role of foreign study as an instrument of developing human resources; the ubiquitous problem of "defection"; the attempts to impute personal or structural reasons for nonreturn; the dilemma of national interests and private rights; the misunderstanding and strain that develop between governments as a result of nonreturn; and the loss felt by the sending country.

The student brain drain and the new migration

Although immigration to the United States since World War II has been far smaller than it was in the nineteenth and early twentieth centuries, it has brought in a population of a different kind, consisting of some of the most highly trained manpower of the sending countries. In recent years, governments around the world have shown increasing concern about the loss, through migration, of many of their best educated citizens. The term *brain drain* captures this shift in character from the migration of "huddled masses yearning to be free" to one of professional and technical workers. The brain drain has been a public policy issue, debated in the halls of the United Nations, the subject of diplomatic confrontations between nations losing manpower and those gaining manpower. Underlying much of this debate has been the assumption that the United States, particularly through its science and technology programs, has been luring foreign manpower to its shores. In effect, it has been proposed that the United States has been "subsidized," in the form of human capital, by some of the very states helped through its foreign aid programs and/or investment by American firms.

As Brinley Thomas has commented, ". . . the diffusion process of the 19th century was based on proletarian mass migration, population-sensitive capital formation and portfolio foreign investment. . . . the scene is now characterized by professional elite migration, science-based capital formation, and direct foreign investment."[5] The migration of the nineteenth century consisted largely of persons in whom their home countries had invested little and who could be expected to produce little. The migrants of the post–World War II period, carrying with them a significant part of their home countries' national wealth in the form of their compatriots' investment in their education, elicit concern. (The legal and illegal influx of less highly trained immigrants from Mexico, and, to a lesser degree, other Latin American countries, does not provoke such indignation on the part of their parent countries.)

Not only has the occupational mix of the migrant population changed; there has been a shift, too, both in the source of migrants and mode of immigration. It is the latter that is the focus of this study. This shift is due in part to changes in United States immigration laws. From 1882 through the 1920s, a series of acts that increasingly restricted migration to persons from Northwestern Europe were passed. However, the McCarran–Walter Act of 1952 introduced a new preference category for immigrants of high educational and occupational quality,[6] as a consequence of which scientists, engineers, and physicians began to migrate in important numbers from less developed countries (LDCs). In 1956, 1,769 "high-level" migrants from the LDCs entered the United States, constituting 32.9 percent of the total migration of scientists, engineers, and physicians for that year. By 1962, there were 2,383 such migrants from the LDCs in the United States – 40 percent of the migration in these categories; after the immigration law was liberalized in 1965, the number and proportion of science, engineering, and medical migrants grew to 7,913 persons, or 51.8 percent of the total.[7]

The new wave of immigration reflects America's new role in international education as well as the liberalization of immigration laws and procedures for a significant proportion of the new migrants who initially entered the United States as temporary visitors, usually students or trainees. In 1967, 23.9 percent of all scientific and technical immigrants had initially entered the United States as students. Thus almost a fourth of the foreign additions to America's stock of high-level technical manpower came through the student route. This mode of migration, although insignificant for the developed countries (accounting for less than 4 percent of the total scientific migration from these countries), is a major source of the manpower from the LDCs. It accounted for 42.6 percent of their total scientific migration to the United States in fiscal 1967.[8]

For 1966 it was estimated that the cost to the United States of educating students from LDCs was 40 million dollars, whereas the cost to their home countries of educating students who migrated to the United States was 88 million dollars. The American educational "aid" program, then, showed a profit of 48 million dollars for that year alone.[9]

As a sociological theme, the new migration presents new research opportunities for social scientists. Because it involves the middle and

upper echelons of a society, our attention must shift away from the
"social problem" focus of so much migration research in the past.[10] We
are not dealing with the "social pathologies" attendant upon, or thought
to be attendant upon, the migration of huddled masses yearning to be
free. If the new migrants constitute a social problem at all, it exists for
their countries of origin rather than that of destination. Their home
countries often perceive their migration as a loss of critical national
assets. That they are considered valuable additions to their new countries is demonstrated in Chapter 6 of this monograph.

This orientation, in turn, forces a reconsideration of the issue of the
brain drain and its causes. As other governments around the world have
expressed their concern, in one way or another, about the migration of
their best and brightest, the finger of blame has been typically pointed
at the wealthy countries of the West, particularly the United States.
With its enormous wealth and government-supported research programs,
the United States has been seen as generating a greater demand for professional and technical workers than it could supply locally, and as
subverting the very international educational exchange programs which
were initiated to increase the scientific, intellectual, and administrative
capacities of the LDCs. In all this discussion, relatively little thought
has been given to the possibility that the student brain drain was at
least in part caused by conditions and policies in the students' home
countries. In so far as the home countries were seen as part of the
"problem," the "fault" was presumed to lie in their relative poverty,
which they could not alter, at least, in the short run.

It is precisely this neglected focus which is the major empirical and
theoretical concern of this monograph. How, and to what extent, do
home country conditions generate the student brain drain? What policies of the students' home countries contribute to the brain drain,
albeit inadvertently? What are the conditions within the students' home
countries that account for the propensity to migrate of particular classes
of persons? And what are the conditions across countries that account
for differences in rates of brain drain? By examining educational systems and occupational opportunity structures, we shall attempt to
answer these questions.

Israel and international student exchange

This volume is devoted to a discussion and analysis of student migration
in the contemporary context, with particular reference to Israelis in the

United States in the 1960s. The choice of Israel as the sending country is based on the author's interest and concern, and the support and help of the officials and citizens of Israel in initiating, developing, and executing the study. The opportunity to work on the project was provided through the initiative of the Israel Government Bureau for Professionals in New York City, whose task it was to help to repatriate as many Israeli students as it could.

In 1956, 71 scientists, engineers, and physicians migrated to the United States from Israel. By 1963, the number of science, engineering, and medical immigrants had grown to 112, and by 1967, there were 206 migrants, of whom 71 – more than one-third – had initially come as students. The science students who became migrants were over one-fourth of the total Israeli student migration for that year.[11] These immigrants were a significant proportion of the new entrants into their respective fields in Israel.

Israel has been a large-scale sender and receiver of students. In 1965, 3,000 Israelis were studying abroad and over 1,000 foreigners were studying in Israeli institutions.[12] Foreign students in Israel were of two kinds: students from the less developed countries of Africa and Asia, and Jewish students from the United States, Western Europe, and Union of South Africa, and Oceana. The presence of students from the less developed world had resulted from an Israeli foreign policy decision to counter the attempts of Arab countries to isolate Israel from its neighbors and the world community at large. Israeli training missions had been located at one time or another in most of the Third World, and students from these countries were brought to Israel at the initiative of the Israeli foreign office.[13]

The decision to welcome Jewish students from the Diaspora precedes the establishment of the State of Israel. When the Hebrew University was founded in Jerusalem in 1925, its mandate included serving as a cultural center for world Jewry, and Diaspora Jewish students have always been found there. In more recent years the programs have expanded, partly in the hope that recruiting Jewish students from abroad would facilitate the migration of Jews from the prosperous countries of the West.

To judge from reports in the Israeli press and discussions with Israelis in all walks of life, Israel's participation in international educational exchange did not have full support in all quarters. The Israeli public, aware of the political character of Israel's educational commitment to Third World nations, often wondered if these efforts were adequately appreciated and worth the heavy expenditure of money, especially when it read of hostile votes in the United Nations. Foreign office personnel felt that they were making an investment for the long run, but the man in the street was often not convinced. By 1973, Israel's educational activities in the LDCs virtually came to an end.

As for Jewish students from abroad, many Israelis have felt that foreigners are given better conditions than Israeli students and that they take places away from Israeli students, who are then forced to study abroad. The attitude toward foreigners thus has related in part to the sense of a scarcity of places for its own student body and concern with the risks entailed in study abroad.

Many Israeli students have sensed that their studying abroad does not meet the unqualified approval of their countrymen at home. Their disquiet has been expressed in excessive justification of study abroad and through direct response to allegations made against them. One student, in a letter to the editor of the major Labor newspaper, wrote in 1966: "The public and the newspapers do us a grave injustice when they describe us as if we left Israel in order to flee from the arduous conditions of Israel, to find wealth in the U.S.A."[14] Another student writing from the United States complained that currently it is believed that those who are studying here (i.e., the United States) are emigrants, or that they did not succeed in Israel and are studying in a football college. Another typical response to the perception of negative sentiments insists that "it is improper to condemn study abroad as long as Israel is not able to offer higher education to all those who seek it."[15]

These perceptions of ambivalence about study abroad seemed to be accurate enough in the 1960s. A journalist who interviewed Israeli students abroad came away with the impression that, "In the main, the Israeli student [who goes abroad to study] feels that he is an 'oddball,' whose sojourn abroad is looked upon unsympathetically."[16] The Israelis who study abroad "are called 'defectors,' 'careerists,' 'money grubbers'; they are looked at with a jaundiced eye. . . ."[17] The complaints against Israeli students abroad were of several types. Some alleged that the Israeli students did not invest enough time presenting Israel's case in its conflict with the Arab nations; others, that "the students preclude all contact with local Jewish communities."[18] Many in Israel who were concerned about maintaining the solidarity of world Jewry felt that the Israeli student abroad had the obligation of maintaining ties with his fellow Jews. Reports from the United States, Switzerland, and the

United Kingdom all indicated that Israelis preferred to stay among themselves and not mix with the local Jewish populations. The issue of this insulation from Diaspora Jewish communities was often interpreted as a reflection on the "Jewishness" of the young generation of Israelis; yet a more perceptive reporter noted that the Israeli students were under great pressure to complete their studies, and often had little money, and so had to work to support themselves. Thus, the contact that they developed with local Jewish communities tended to become instrumental relationships, as when Jewish communities engaged the Israeli students as teachers, youth leaders, etc.

But the central concern and source of criticism leveled at Israeli study abroad has been the issue of migration. Israeli attitudes toward migration are embedded in the Hebrew language. Migration *into* Israel is called *aliyah* (i.e., "going up"); migration *out of* Israel is called *yeridah* (i.e., "going down"). Migrants out of Israel are called *yordim,* a term of opprobrium and moral condemnation. Those who migrate are seen as casting a vote against the Third Jewish Commonwealth. Nonreturning students represented a serious threat to the primary moral ideal of the State of Israel. One journalist wrote, "Israel is a country of in-migration not out-migration; therefore, migration from other countries is not comparable to that which occurs from Israel."[19] This is a pervasive theme in discussions of Israelis abroad. Although it may have undergone modification in recent years, it was particularly acute in the mid 1960s.

Yet, despite the heated discussion of the problem of study abroad in the Israeli press, no one actually knew very much about its dimensions.

A large body of research on foreign students was already available at the time that this study was launched. In the 1950s, the Social Science Research Council had sponsored a series of monographs on foreign students, with the primary focus on attitude change "toward members of racial, religious, or national groups in situations of intergroup contact."[20] An excellent bibliography published in 1962 listed ninety-nine doctoral dissertations and master's essays based on research about foreign students. Of these dissertations and essays, only two dealt directly with the problem of student migration; the others were concerned with psychosocial adjustments in the United States.[21] (The brain drain was apparently a problem of the 1960s.) Some of the speculative literature was suggestive, but the state of empirically grounded knowledge of the issues was inadequate. The Israel Government Bureau for Professionals of the Israel Ministry of Labor, in an effort to suggest policies that the government might adopt to bring more students home, commissioned a study of the situation to determine the number of students in the United States, their reasons for coming here, and the factors that brought them back home or caused them to migrate. Israel felt that it needed this information to develop appropriate public policy.

Basic sociological problems associated with the brain drain

The public policy agenda of Israel and of the other nations involved raises a set of analytic problems that has been the subject of research and theoretical concern within sociology; these problems are the major analytic foci of this study. First is the study of migration per se. What are the determinants and consequences of migration for different populations? How do individuals decide to migrate? What are some of the social structural facts that influence their decisions? How do these facts vary from population to population? What is the differential effect of these facts among various populations?

Second, a growing body of theory and research has focused on the school systems as key agents in the allocation and distribution of life chances. These life chances, in turn, relate to questions of social and geographic mobility of the participants and reflect as well upon the social structures in which the actors perform. The study of mobility in modern societies is in large measure the study of the social sources and consequences of educational opportunity structures and of individual performance within school systems. The schools serve as "gatekeepers" for the educational system and for the larger society as well. In this study, we shall be extending that focus to that of geographic mobility in a world arena. Theoretically, then, this study is as much one of educational systems as it is of migration, and, most particularly, it is a study of the articulation of several societal subsystems and their impact on migration decisions. The empirical data come from questionnaires completed by individuals, and thus the empirical unit of analysis is the individual and aggregates of individuals. The explicandum is their migration decision; the explicans will be sought in the social structures of their nations. In effect, we are using social structure to explain migration, and using migration as a window onto social structure. Among the broad range of entities termed social structure, we are particularly interested in the educational system and in the professional opportunity structure.

The third major question is that of social intervention. Given the constraints set by ongoing complex social systems, what are the "leverages" available for influencing behavior? Specifically, what are the policy alternatives open to the governments involved and how do we measure the effectiveness of policies that are in operation or contemplated? What are the social costs and benefits of various policy alternatives? What are the methodologies appropriate for the measurement of costs and benefits?

In the next chapter (Chapter 2), we examine the ways in which the Israeli educational system influences the students' decisions to study in the United States. The analysis focuses on the students' motives for study abroad and shows how these motives are shaped by success or failure in the Israeli educational system. Following that, in Chapter 3, the interrelationships of academic performance, employment opportunities in Israel, and repatriation are analyzed. A model is developed for tracing the effects of academic achievement on the Israeli professional occupational opportunity structure and the variations in major sectors of Israeli society. Chapter 4 describes Israeli and American brain-drain policies and suggests alternative policies. In Chapter 5, we generalize to other foreign student groups the model developed to account for Israelis in the United States. In the last chapter (Chapter 6), we examine some of the implications of study abroad and migration for educational and development policies of the nations involved.

2. Coming to America

In 1961, the Institute of International Education (IIE) reported that there were 877 Israeli students attending American colleges and universities. By 1964, the IIE census counted 1,382 Israelis, and in 1966-7 the number had grown to 1,878. There were hundreds of other Israelis enrolled in training programs in American industry, hospitals, and government.

America has been the major destination for Israelis studying abroad. French statistics for 1966-7 show that only 218 Israelis were enrolled, whereas British statistics indicate that 241 Israelis matriculated during 1967-8. The expatriate Israeli student population in the United States is a heterogeneous group. They are to be found in all the major universities in the United States, with particularly heavy representation in California and the New York–Boston "megalopolis." They are enrolled in virtually all the disciplines represented in the American university, with substantial proportions in natural science, social science, and engineering. In terms of academic quality, one can find in their midst both scholars and dilettantes.

What is there about the United States and Israel (and most particularly, what is there about the school system of the two countries) which brings so many Israelis of such varying background and competence to the United States? One way of answering these questions is to ask students to explain their behavior in such a way that their explanations and reasons for study abroad would reflect on the constraints set by Israeli society, particularly the structure of opportunity within the Israeli educational system. Analysis of student reasons or motives for study abroad then becomes an examination of the impact of two school systems on the lives of the students. By way of introduction to the analysis of the motives of Israeli students and the educational opportunity structures, we turn briefly to a review of some findings on motives for study abroad.

Prior research concerning motives for study abroad: who studies abroad and why do they go?

A host of factors has been proposed to explain why students go abroad. It has been suggested that some of those who do so have been inadequate students at home and that foreign universities, often unable to evaluate records from abroad, have accepted students who were not college material.[1] Other students are trapped by the small size of their national universities; that is, their records ought to permit them to enter a good university at home, but facilities simply do not exist.[2] There are others, particularly the sons of the local aristocracy or upper class, who see study abroad as either a lark or as a kind of "finishing school." For them, the foreign diploma is a mark of social prestige rather than of academic accomplishment.[3] For some, ambitions outstrip local facilities; their interests cannot be met at home simply because their subject is not taught or is inadequately taught.

Given the decision to study abroad, why does the student choose to come to the United States? As will be shown in Chapter 5, the choice of country in which to study is influenced by the student's intellectual and occupational interests and his nation's cultural traditions. The latter, in turn, often reflect the colonial history of the various countries involved: Students from former British colonies tend to go to the United Kingdom; Francophone Africans to France, and so forth. These students usually have some knowledge of the language and traditions of the former imperial power and adapt more readily to its universities. A large proportion of the foreign students in American universities are citizens of America's client states. Further, because the United States is the world's technological leader, the proportion of foreign students in technological fields is greater for the United States than for any other industrial nation.[4]

Some students choose to come to the United States because they have been told by their compatriots that one can support oneself by working part time, an option that is not as readily available elsewhere in the world. This factor is particularly important for the Israelis. The scarcity of skilled manpower in the field of Jewish education affords many Israelis opportunities for part-time employment so that they can subsist in the United States even without the aid of fellowships. Comparable opportunities are not available to them in Europe.

There is another group who, in a sense, are not bona fide students at all, but rather immigrants who see their student visa as the first step in acquiring citizenship or at least permanent residence in the United States. They often drift from school to school, frequently one jump ahead of the immigration officials, until they are compelled to leave the country, or through marriage or other legal devices are able to remain in the United States. Immigration, whether covert or overt, presents particularly agonizing moral dilemmas for Israelis. The young Israeli who wishes to leave the country permanently or for a long sojourn must legitimate his trip in terms of national needs if he is to avoid the negative sanctions that are applied to those whom the Israelis call *yordim.* The student status supplies such legitimation for the Israeli who wishes to go abroad.

Study abroad can perform many functions for the individual student and his country. However, in the main, students are moved to study abroad by academic and professional considerations, along with personal desire to see the world and test themselves under new and different conditions. The students' reasons for study abroad can be understood as responses to the Israeli educational system and Israeli society more generally. Through an analysis of their expressed reasons for study abroad, we will attempt to understand those aspects of Israeli society that shape their reasons.

The empirical study of reasons

Why Israelis come to the United States as students is obviously related to other questions, among which is their choice of occupation. Not all occupations require higher education. Why did they choose a given occupation that requires higher education, which, in turn, brought them to the United States? One could engage in a fruitless infinite regress by asking "why" for every reason given. We will take the student's occupational choice and his being in the United States on student status as givens, and examine the motives for being here in terms of Israeli educational and social structure.

In studying reasons or motives, one must distinguish first between official and private reasons. The sponsors of educational exchange (if one takes the public statements of policy seriously) are concerned with issues that students rarely mention. Some policy makers have talked of increasing international understanding; others of inhibiting the development of world communism; still others of developing human capital. It may well be that educational exchange does perform these and other functions which correspond with official motives. However, qualitative interviews with the students have demonstrated that the official motives for promoting and supporting educational exchange are unrelated to the expressed motives of the students.

Second, it is crucial that we distinguish motives, either public or private, from consequences or functions. We are interested in the motives of which the actor is aware and which he feels have caused him to do what he has done. Last, the analysis is restricted to motives that may be understood in the light of the facts of social life in Israel and the United States and the position of the students in the two societies.

In most cross-sectional survey analysis, the dependent variable is the performance versus nonperformance of an act, which in this instance might mean distinguishing between students who did and did not decide to study abroad. By contrast, a *reason analysis* attempts to distinguish among types of actors, all of whom have performed the act in question. In reason analysis, the analyst examines the several paths that have led to the same act. This is the procedure followed in the present study. All the members of the population had come to the United States and have been students here some time during their sojourn in the United States. Our task is to distinguish their motives in theoretically fruitful ways.

In order to study motives systematically, one must first develop what is called an "accounting scheme." This delimits the areas of interest to some finite set of factors believed to be significant for a segment of the population. The dimensions of the accounting scheme should distinguish elements in the population studied and should be explicable in terms of the social situations of the members of the population. To account for the motives of Israeli students in the United States, an accounting scheme consisting of five dimensions was developed. These dimensions are

    (a) perceived superiority of the American academic system,

    (b) academic financial facilitation (stipends and scholarships),

    (c) perceived or real inability to enter Israeli university,

    (d) nonacademic financial facilitation,

    (e) nonacademic reasons.

The first four of these dimensions largely take into account the effects of the Israeli educational system on shaping the motives of students abroad. The last dimension refers to the more general impact of the student's position in Israeli society. For each dimension, a set of questions was developed to give concrete operational meaning to the rather abstract accounting scheme dimension. The accounting scheme, then, is the first part of a microtheory of motives for a particular population.

The respondents were presented with a list of twenty-four reasons for coming to the United States and were asked to indicate which of these reasons were applicable to themselves. Those who indicated that they came because their parents migrated to the United States were removed from the entire study population. Those who said they came because their spouse decided to study in the United States were removed from the reason analysis on the grounds that they did not themselves engage in a decision process. The analysis proper, then, begins with twenty-two reasons that were developed as indicators of the five dimensions of the accounting scheme.

If we were to handle each reason dichotomously and generate all of the logically possible patterns of reasons, we would arrive at 2^{22} or 4,194,304 distinct patterns of reasons – a clearly unmanageable situation! If we were to operate with the five dimensions as variables and again define each of them dichotomously, we would generate a property space containing 2^5 or 32 possible cells, which is a considerable improvement over the 2^{22} situation but still rather cumbersome. Further, by immediately moving from the twenty-two individual items to the five dimensions, we would be assuming that the items actually do fit the accounting-scheme model. Thus, both for reasons of determining the fit between the model of the accounting scheme and the empirical relationship of the items, and to attempt further reduction of the property space, a correlation matrix of the items was developed. Using a factoring procedure, it was found that the five dimensions of the accounting scheme could be reduced to three primary clusters, in which six of the items were removed because they were not clearly classifiable into any cluster or dimension.[5] The relationships among the items and the clusters which they form are presented in Figure 2.1.

The relative distance of an item from any other item or set of items is determined by the correlation between or among those items.[6] Thus, students who report that their relatives promised financial aid are extremely unlikely to report having received a scholarship from either the Israeli or American governments. They are also unlikely to express a motivated desire to gain professional experience. They are quite likely,

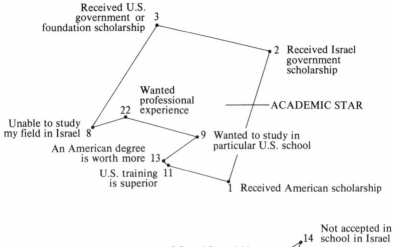

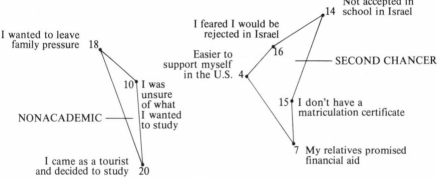

Figure 2.1 Multidimensional scaling plot of reasons for studying in the United States.

though, to have been rejected (or to have feared they would be rejected) by a university in Israel.

Items that are connected by solid lines constitute a cluster of empirically related responses. The Academic Star cluster indicates that the student came to the United States because of the inherent desirability of American education or training in his field. The Second Chancer cluster indicates either outright inability or perceived inability to acquire a higher education in Israel. The emphasis in the Academic Star cluster is on American academic pull, whereas the Second Chancer cluster suggests Israeli academic push. These two clusters are treated as mutually exclusive in the analysis that follows. The third cluster, Nonacademic, does not reflect the academic situation either in Israel or in the United States, and this pattern of motives will be shown to be a function of largely nonacademic elements in the student's life.

In the course of the analysis, groups of students will be termed Academic Stars, Second Chancers, and Nonacademics. The categories are derived from the reasons the students have given for coming to the United States, but they also reflect the structural factors behind those reasons and represent distinct paths of opportunity as well as distinct types of students. The Academic Star hopes to enhance his success with an education abroad and often has an institutional source of support. The Second Chancer is seeking elsewhere for opportunities that seem to be closed to him at home. It is the purpose of the analysis to show more precisely how the educational (and more generally social) processes and structures generate types of motives for those who come to study in the United States.

Organization of Israeli education and its impact on students' reasons for going abroad

The Israeli educational system is based on a mixture of public and private initiative, and on populist and elitist educational doctrine and practice. The basic pattern of education in Israel antedates the establishment of the state. Under the British mandate, the Jewish community of Palestine, with some limited help from the mandatory government, supported a system of education through high school. The university system was created and supported in partnership with the Jewish community in the Diaspora.

After independence was established in 1948, the basic pattern of education was maintained. The Education Act of 1949 made the voluntary system of universal education both compulsory and free. High school education has been supported in part by the central government, in part by local government (municipalities), and is in part dependent on tuition fees.

Some form of elementary education is available for the entire population in Israel. The elitist pattern shows itself most clearly at the secondary level. The comprehensive high school, which is characteristic of American secondary education, is unknown in Israel. Until recently, in moving from the eighth grade to high school, the student either chose or was assigned to one of several secondary school options, among which the academic high school was the major road to higher education.

Data analyzed for the period 1950–7 shows the following pattern of tracking and dropout from the first grade to entrance into the system of higher education:

Of every 100 who entered elementary school, 84 completed the eighth grade (maximum estimate).

Of every 100 who completed the eighth grade, 73 went on to some secondary education, of whom 34 entered nonacademic secondary schools, and 39 an academic secondary school.

Of every 100 who entered an academic secondary school, 51 reached the twelfth grade and 48, that is, 16 percent, sat for the matriculation exam.

Of every 100 boys who passed the matriculation examination, 90 entered university.

Of every 100 girls who passed the matriculation examination, 80 entered university.

More recent data on the proportion of the total population entering twelfth grade in an academic high school show an increase from 9.8 percent in 1959 to 13.5 percent in 1963. However, the pattern emphasized in this study – the progressive restrictions in opportunity, and the relatively small proportion of all students entering college – remains apparent.[7]

The Israeli educational system offers little in the way of second chances for those who do not make the grade the first time around. The winnowing out of the academically weaker students begins in the eighth grade and continues throughout their term in the university. Some of the winnowing process continues on into the universities on the basis of the student's grade-point average. The higher it is, the less likely he is to be a Second Chancer.

The student population in our study reflected these factors in the Israeli educational structure. Among those with academic reasons for being in the United States and who had not earned any degree in Israel, 52 percent were Second Chancers, whereas for those who already held an Israeli bachelor's degree the comparable figure was 11 percent, and for those with a graduate degree it was 4 percent. That is, over half the Israelis who had come to the United States as undergraduates did so because, by their own lights, they had not succeeded in the Israeli educational system.

Thus, the major difference in patterns of motives corresponds largely to the students' graduate or undergraduate status and, in turn, can be traced to students' experiences in the educational system at least as far back as the point of movement from the primary school to secondary school.

In Israel, most primary school pupils are enrolled either in state-secular or state-religious schools. There is some difference in "mood" and curriculum of these schools, but students are undifferentiated as to occupational or educational destinations. Since high school attendance is neither compulsory nor free, a rather large proportion of the pupils stop their education at the end of junior high school. For those who expect to be college bound, it has been crucial that they be enrolled in an academic high school. The vocational high schools particularly (and to some extent the agricultural schools) train students directly for jobs, whereas the academic high school, modeled after the European gymnasium, has had university preparation as its primary concern.

At the time of this study, students completing primary school and planning a secondary education were still being placed in the appropriate high school on the basis of their performance on an examination, called the *seker*, which was given during the eighth grade.

Being placed in a nonacademic high school, in turn, limited access to higher education in Israel. This is reflected in the relationship between type of high school attended and reasons for coming to the United States (Table 2.1). Until recent changes in the system of college admissions, which have made the matriculation examination more flexible, access to higher education was controlled by the high school. The matriculation examination is taken as a matter of course by students in the twelfth grade in academic high schools. Some of the agricultural high schools have prepared students for the matriculation examinations, but few of the vocational students have taken it. Although recent modifications now encourage several thousand Israeli students to take the matriculation examination each year as external students, data for the period covered by our study show the overwhelming importance of the examination in the 1960s.

During the academic year 1966–7, among students in the universities in Israel, 75 percent held a standard Israeli matriculation certificate, 11 percent had passed the examination as external students, (i.e., outside the regular secondary school structure), 10 percent held a foreign matriculation certification, and 4 percent held some other certificate.[8] Ex-

Table 2.1. *Reason for study in the United States by type of high school attended (percentages)*

Reason for study in the U.S.	Academic	Agricultural	Externe[a]	Vocational	Other[b]	Abroad
Academic Star	71	62	53	40	56	65
Second Chancer	26	34	43	58	42	35
No academic reason	3	5	5	2	2	0
N (no. in subgroup)	(734)	(110)	(89)	(134)	(273)	(109)

$$\chi^2 = 72.56; \ df = 10; \ p < .001$$

Note: All chi-square tests reported throughout this volume are one tail.
[a] Matriculation examination not taken in course.
[b] Normal schools, *yeshivot,* and not elsewhere classified.

cluding those who held a foreign matriculation certificate, 95 percent of the students in universities in Israel held an Israeli matriculation certificate, which in the vast majority of cases was earned in course, whereas among those studying in the United States the comparable figure was 79 percent. Among the Israeli students in the United States who held a matriculation certificate, 26 percent were Second Chancers, as compared with 60 percent of those without a matriculation certificate.

The effect of the matriculation certificate within each major type of secondary school on subsequent study abroad career plans is shown in Table 2.2 The difference in patterns of motives between those who had attended academic and agricultural schools is fully explained by the differential likelihood of having earned matriculation certificate in the two school types. In the case of the vocational schools, the difference is in part explained by the matriculation certificate, but a significant difference remains.

Holding a matriculation certificate has been for practical purposes a necessary but not sufficient condition for entrance into university in Israel. Because demand for university places has consistently exceeded the supply, the candidate for admission to university in Israel has been competing with his fellow students for scarce places, which have been allocated on the basis of grades on the matriculation examination, and, in certain faculties, an entrance examination (termed a *concourse*) given over and above the matriculation examination.

As Table 2.3 shows, the lower the student's grades on the matricula-

Table 2.2. *Reason for study in the United States by matriculation certificate and by type of high school attended (percentages)*

Reason for study in the U.S.	Academic: matriculation certificate		Agricultural: matriculation certificate		Vocational: matriculation certificate	
	Yes	No	Yes	No	Yes	No
Academic Star	74	43	76	40	52	29
Second Chancer	23	55	20	56	46	69
No academic reason	3	2	5	5	2	3
N (no. in subgroup)	(671)	(58)	(66)	(43)	(48)	(80)
	χ^2 = 29.75 df = 2 $p <$ .001		χ^2 = 15.56 df = 2 $p <$ .001		χ^2 = 7.01 df = 2 $p <$ .05	

Table 2.3. *Reason for study in the United States by matriculation examination score among respondents holding an Israeli matriculation certificate (percentages)*

Reason for study in the U.S.	Matriculation examination score:			
	9–10	8–8.5	7–7.5	6–6.5
Academic Star	87	79	63	53
Second Chancer	12	18	33	42
No academic reason	1	3	4	5
N (no. in subgroup)	(96)	(385)	(424)	(115)
	χ^2 = 54.10; df = 6; $p <$ .001			

tion examination, the more likely he is to indicate that he came to the United States because his way was blocked in Israel. The educational system is intellectually meritocratic. This is a theme to which we shall have occasion to return later on in the analysis. Table 2.3 suggests also that academic achievement is positively related to academic motives. The lower the level of achievement reported on the matriculation examination, the more likely is the student to report that he was motivated solely by nonacademic factors in coming to the United States.

Because the matriculation examination is largely geared to an academic curriculum, those who have taken the matriculation examination without adequate secondary school preparation are likely to show a lower level of performance on the examination. Among graduates of the academic high schools, 53 percent reported an average matriculation examination score of 8 or above, whereas for vocational school graduates the comparable figure is 32 percent. Among those who have taken the examination as external students, the figure is 19 percent. Part of the difference in pattern of motives between academic and vocational school graduates is accounted for by their grades on the matriculation examination.[9]

The effect of the type of high school attended on the patterns of motives of Israeli students in the United States is presented in Tables 2.1, 2.2, and 2.3. Taking the extreme cases, vocational high school graduates were far more likely to have been Second Chancers than their colleagues with academic high school diplomas. The difference between the two types of school is 32 percentage points. In Table 2.2 the difference was reduced to 14 percentage points among students without a matriculation certificate, and 23 percentage points among those with a matriculation certificate. In Table 2.4, taking into account the students' grades on the matriculation examination in the academic and vocational trends, the difference is reduced to 18 percentage points.[10]

It is a well-established regularity that social class of origin predicts level of academic achievement and success. Lower-class students tend to show higher rates of dropout; when they continue on in school, they tend to be enrolled in the less prestigious schools or track. The continu-

Table 2.4. *Reason for study in the United States by type of high school, standardized on matriculation examination score (percentages)*

Reason for study in the U.S.	Academic	Vocational
Academic Star	72	60
Second Chancer	21	39
No academic reason	4	1
N (no. in subgroup)	(671)	(48)

$\chi^2 = 9.42$; df = 2; $p < .01$

ing effect of social origins on educational opportunity and performance creates dilemmas for the Israeli educational planner. Free or subsidized education is one of the ways in which Israel (and other countries) redistribute wealth and life chances. Despite its commitment to social equality, there is a smaller proportion of lower-class Israelis in academic high schools and universities. The amount of "social bias" in Israel is small as compared with other countries, but it does exist. Generally, it has been found that the lower the age of tracking, the greater the social bias. The key tracking point for the Israelis was the eighth (and is now the ninth) grade, whereas for many other countries de facto tracking occurs earlier in the elementary grades.[11]

The Israeli educational planner is interested in maximizing the intellectual resources of his country. His job is to allocate students to that track which will best utilize their talents both for the national welfare and their personal fulfillment. If that investment is to have maximum payoff in terms of the productivity of the populace, then the tracking of students should not take into account intellectually irrelevant social class effects.

Social class of origin predicts the students' motives for studying in the United States (Table 2.5, A). The relationship between social class and motive for study abroad is a function of the relationship between social class and educational achievement. The higher the social class of origin, the more likely the student is to have earned a degree in Israel. Although the relationship between social class and having earned an undergraduate degree in Israel holds for the study population as a whole, it is reduced considerably for those who attended an academic high school in Israel (Table 2.5, B).

As previously noted, tracking into high school is a key determinant of college admissions in Israel and, hence, of motives for studying abroad, because the social class effect on motives for study abroad is largely a function of the type of high school attended. Although attending an academic high school is a function of social class (Table 2.5, C), among those who did attend an academic high school, social class has little or no effect on their subsequent performance, for example, their likelihood of having completed high school or their grades on the matriculation examination (Table 2.5, D). The relationship between social class and motives for studying in the United States exists largely as a consequence of the tracking system. If the student has entered an academic secondary school, social class effects largely disappear in this population.

Table 2.5. *Reason for study in the United States and several measures of academic achievement in Israel by social class origins*

	Social class as measured by father's highest level of education		
	Primary school	High school	College or university
A. Reason for study in the U.S. (% who are Second Chancers):	40 (451)[a]	37 (649)	28 (465)	χ^2 = 15.99 df = 2 p < .001
B. Highest degree earned in Israel, in total population (%):				
No degree	72	67	59	χ^2 = 18.28
Bachelor's	17	18	23	df = 4
Graduate	12	16	19	p < .001
	(451)	(649)	(465)	
Among those who attended academic high school in Israel (%):				
No degree	55	57	50	χ^2 = 5.11
Bachelor's	29	23	27	df = 4
Graduate	17	20	23	p < .3
	(161)	(287)	(268)	
C. % Attended academic high school:	36 (451)	44 (649)	58 (465)	χ^2 = 46.68 df = 2 p < .001
D. Of those who attended academic high school:				
% Completed	96 (161)	93 (287)	96 (268)	χ^2 = 3.20 df = 2 p < .2
% Earned grade of 8 or above on matriculation examination	49 (144)	50 (261)	53 (251)	χ^2 = .67 df = 2 p < .7

[a] In this table and all tables in this chapter, numbers in parentheses are subgroup *N*s.

Career choice specialization and
reason for study abroad

From 1961 through 1964 the number of places in all Israeli institutions of higher learning increased at an annual rate of 20 percent; however, the rate of increase in science and technology was only 10 percent.[12] The much smaller rate of increase in the number of students admitted into the faculties of natural science and engineering is not a consequence of lack of student interest in these fields; it is the result of administrative decisions that have resulted in restricted access to these faculties. A far larger proportion of academically qualified students are rejected in the faculties of natural science and engineering.[13] The situation in medicine has been the most critical; it had been estimated (prior to the opening of a new medical school associated with Tel Aviv University) that only one in six applicants was accepted.[14] (The United States, however, is not an alternative for students who have not been accepted into Israeli medical schools. This is discussed in greater detail in the following.)

It is difficult to know exactly to what factor or factors the different patterns of growth in the several faculties may be attributed. On the one hand, the humanities have historically been favored in Israeli higher education.[15] Costs per student also vary considerably by faculty, with humanities, law, and social science being the cheapest to run, and medicine, mathematics and natural science, and engineering the most expensive.[16] If the intent of expansion was simply to increase the number of places in universities, without regard to manpower needs, expanding those fields with the least cost per additional student would be a sensible approach. However, it is impossible to know whether it was cultural tradition or economic calculation that influenced Israeli educational planners most in mapping out this uneven expansion. Whatever the cause, fewer students are rejected in the "soft" fields. Is the American "second chance" then, more characteristic of students in the "hard" fields of medicine, natural science, and engineering?

Of the three fields in which the demand for places far exceeds the supply, engineering alone shows a marked difference in the pattern of reasons among the students (Table 2.6). As to medicine, although it is a very crowded field in Israel, the United States has not been, at least in recent years, a center for doctoral studies in medicine for aliens. The Israeli who cannot enter a medical school in Israel turns to Switzerland, Austria, or Italy. Between 1951 and 1963, American medical schools

Table 2.6. *Reason for study in the United States by field of study (percentages)*

Reason for study in the U.S.	Busi- ness	Medi- cine	Social science	Natural science, mathe- matics	Human- ities, education, the arts	Engi- neer- ing
Academic Star	71	76	68	68	65	50
Second Chancer	26	24	31	31	28	48
No academic reason	3	—	2	2	7	2
N (no. in subgroup)	(180)	(86)	(235)	(271)	(230)	(527)

$$\chi^2 = 76.39; df = 10; p < .001$$

had only 1,200 foreign students (i.e., 1 percent of the medical school population) of whom 2 percent were Israelis.[17] The total of 24 Israeli students over this time span averages out to less than 2 Israelis a year. Israelis studying medicine in the United States are, for the most part, premedical or postdoctoral students. Although both natural science and engineering faculties in Israel severely restrict entrance, engineering alone shows a pattern significantly different from those of the other fields. It is not simply lack of educational opportunity in Israel that brings students to the United States but also the wealth of such opportunities here.

The problem of the engineering students is not merely a matter of supply and demand for university places. Among the Second Chancers, those who were would-be engineers had weaker academic backgrounds and had attended the academically weaker high schools. Only 29 percent of the students who had attended academic high schools planned engineering careers, whereas 69 percent of those who had attended vocational high schools planned to be engineers. In our study, engineers were less likely to have the basic matriculation document without which entrance into the Technion (the Israel Institute of Technology) is almost impossible. Beyond that, even among those who did hold a matriculation certificate, engineers tended to have lower scores on the matriculation examinations, holding constant the type of high school attended. Among those who had attended an academic high school, 62 percent of the natural scientists had scored 8 or better on their matriculation examinations, whereas for engineers the comparable figure was only 46 percent. Taking into account the academic achievement of engineers and natural scientists, much of the variation in motivational patterns across the two fields is accounted for by their different levels of accomplishment. This comparison is presented in Table 2.7.

Israeli education is organized to produce specialists. On the university level, the student is required to study two majors. The broad-based liberal arts background, which is characteristic of American education, is unknown in Israel (although there are some who have wanted to move Israeli higher education in that direction). Specialization is characteristic of the high school system as well. At the end of the tenth grade in the academic high schools, the student must choose a *megama* ("academic major"). The basic majors are *realit* (i.e., physical sciences and mathematics), biological sciences (which is rather similar to the *realit* option in terms of its emphasis on natural science and mathematics), humanities, and social science.

In the main, the student's choice of university subject(s) is consistent with his high school major. However, what is the result of a shift in interest? Does the student who has emphasized the sciences in high school find himself at a loss if he later decides on the humanities or social sciences? To what degree, if any, is a student at a disadvantage when he changes his field of interest between high school and college?

Table 2.7. *Reason for study in the United States, among academic high school graduates, by matriculation examination grades and field of study (percentages)*

Reason for study in the U.S.	Grade of 7.5 and less		Grade of 8 and over	
	Engineering	Natural science	Engineering	Natural science
Academic Star	51	64	80	83
Second Chancer	45	32	20	16
No academic reason	4	2	0	1
N (no. in subgroup)	(103)	(50)	(89)	(81)
	$\chi^2 = 2.66$		$\chi^2 = 0.09$	
	df = 2		df = 2	
	$p < .3$		$p < .8$	

Table 2.8. *Reason for study in the United States, among academic high school graduates, by field of study and by high school major (percentages who are Second Chancers)*

	High school major	
Field of study	Humanities and social sciences	Realit and biological sciences
Engineering and natural sciences	33 (48)	30 (279)
Humanities and social sciences	27 (128)	17 (63)
Significance within categories of high school majors:		
Humanities and social sciences	$\chi^2 = 0.35$ df $= 1$ $p < .6$	
Realit and biological sciences	$\chi^2 = 3.49$ df $= 1$ $p < .05$	

The student who wants to shift from the humanities and social sciences to the natural sciences and engineering in college will face difficulty. The student who shifts in the opposite direction finds that his chances have actually improved (Table 2.8)

Some nonacademic reasons for study abroad

In reviewing other studies on the determinants of schooling abroad, we found both academic and nonacademic reasons cited. For most Israelis, whether they come to enhance their present advantages or to broaden their opportunities, study abroad is motivated by clear academic and professional considerations. Few young Israelis can afford the luxury of an extended period abroad without a clear academic goal. By the time they are ready for university they have spent two, three, or more years in the army and are anxious to get on with their careers. To go abroad without professional purpose is a form of self-indulgence that Israel does not suffer gladly.

Table 2.9. *Nonacademic reasons for coming to the United States, by social attributes*

	% Giving nonacademic reasons for coming to the U.S.	
Age of Arrival:		
25 or under	27	χ^2 = 37.33
	(921)	df = 1
26 or over	14	$p <$ .001
	(655)	
Marital status on arrival:		
Not married	27	χ^2 = 87.49
	(515)	df = 1
Married	9	$p <$ .001
	(1067)	
Sex:		
Female	34	χ^2 = 28.34
	(266)	df = 1
Male	19	$p <$ .001
	(1409)	

There is a relatively small group of Israeli students, however, who see educational exchange as a means of leaving an uncomfortable situation at home and an opportunity to see the world as well. We had identified these students as the Nonacademics. Members of the nonacademic community may or may not have some academic reason for studying abroad. As was shown in Figure 2.1, when they do have some academic reason for coming to the United States, they could be classified as Second Chancers. The determinants of Nonacademics, however, are more broadly social rather than educational. These students are more likely to be female, young, and unmarried (Table 2.9). They have less in the way of professional and familial commitments and responsibilities of their own and are more likely to be subject to social pressures in Israel from which they would like to escape. Only 6 percent of the older married male students as compared with 42 percent of the younger unmarried female students are members of the Nonacademic group. Student status gives them the legal right to remain in the United States and the moral right to remain out of Israel.

Summary

The Israeli students' expressed purposes for study in the United States reflect the relationship between the American and Israeli educational opportunity structures.

Until recent changes in the Israeli educational system encouraged more students to take the "external" matriculation and established university courses for students without it, the academic high school was virtually one's only chance for a professional career. By contrast, in the United States there is the opportunity for second, third, and more beginnings. Thus, the wide range of entrance requirements and academic standards in American colleges and universities has offered opportunities to students tracked out of higher education in Israel. American schools are also more flexible in regard to formal requirements for admission. The weak student is usually able to find some provincial American college that would be glad to have foreign students as evidence of the school's cosmopolitan character.

For the superior student, America offers other advantages, for example, a high level of graduate education which may not be available at home. The very size of the United States permits a degree of subject matter specialization that smaller countries cannot afford to offer, certainly not at the level of academic quality that superior graduate students would want and would be able to appreciate and assimilate.

The Israeli student's place in the American academic system and his motives for study abroad are conditioned by his academic history in Israel. Tracking decisions made when the students were fourteen or fifteen years old have dictated their motives some ten years later. In the next chapter, we follow up this theme and examine the relationships among success in school, the occupational structure, and migration.

3. Education and economic opportunity

So many factors can be adduced to account for migration decisions that one cannot capture all of them – all the sentiments, influences, values, and structural factors that predispose an individual to migrate or return home. Obviously, Israelis who are happy in Israel will be more likely to return home, whereas those who are unhappy are more likely to migrate.[1] To list a series of attitudes that correlate with and predict migration would not particularly help us understand the socially structured determinants of migration behavior. We are primarily concerned with the ways in which Israeli social structure shapes and patterns migration propensities. Within the social structure, we are particularly concerned with the educational system as a determinant of opportunities and perceptions of opportunities.

One of the key issues that all social systems face is that of allocating and distributing social roles, facilities, and rewards. In the development from traditional to modern society, the criterion of allocation shifted from ascription to achievement. The ideal of modern societies has been to each according to his merit; however, establishing merit is always a difficult problem, particularly during the early stages of a career. Educational systems, which train for social and economic roles, play a significant role in establishing and certifying merit, thus controlling access to professional opportunity.[2]

In the previous chapter we analyzed the planned formal system of allocation *within* the educational system and its consequences for the decision to go abroad. In this chapter we will show that the propensity to return to Israel is a function of the student's position in the professional opportunity structure and that the student's position in the opportunity structure, in turn, is a function of relative success in the school system in Israel. We will show how the achievement-oriented, Israeli, professional opportunity structure works so as to repatriate the best Israeli students. The schools will be shown to be a major gatekeeper for Israeli society and, thus, to play a central role in shaping the student's migration decision.

The chapter addresses itself to three problems. First, paralleling Chapter 2, we present and validate an operational measure of migration. Second, we develop an estimate of the true rate of the Israeli student brain drain. Third, we develop a set of models that enables us to examine the ways in which the school system influences migration decisions.

Intention and behavior: validating the indicator

Commonsensically, an immigrant is a person who has taken up permanent residence in another country. The problem, of course, is to determine what constitutes permanent residence. The Israelis who were part of the study population were all resident in the United States. How do we know whether their residence in the United States is to be permanent or temporary? There is no way of being absolutely sure in every instance except in retrospect at the end of their lives. The most obvious approach is to ask the students directly whether or not they expect to return home.

When asked whether or not they expected to return home, 51 percent of the population then resident in the United States indicated that they did expect to return home.

The obvious advantage of the direct question lies precisely in the simplicity and directness of the approach. Who should know better what students expect to do than the students themselves? The disadvantage lies in the students' possible inability or unwillingness to answer the question truthfully. From the answers to the questions themselves, we do not know whether they are responding in terms of what they think they should be saying or whether they are, in fact, reporting their plans as best they know them. In short, is the statement that the student expects to return home (or remain in the United States) to be taken at face value as an indicator of his actual behavior sometime in the future?

The first check on the data is an internal comparison juxtaposing the statements of intention alongside the self-reported legal status of the students. The majority of students entered the United States on one of the educational visas. These visas are part of the general class of visas available for *temporary visitors.* Persons with temporary visitors' visas may not stay in the United States permanently. In order to remain permanently in the United States legally, the temporary visitor must adjust his status to that of *permanent resident,* and ultimately he becomes an American citizen.

The estimates of the magnitude of the student brain drain presented in the introductory chapter were generated by congressional committees and were based on visa adjustment tabulations made by the Immigration and Naturalization Service of the Department of Justice. The exact nature of these visa categories will be discussed in detail in Chapter 4. For the moment we can take the adjustment figures as prima facie legal evidence of migration. Table 3.1, A presents the relationship between stated intentions and legal status for all of those who entered on educational visas (i.e., F or J visas; see Chapter 4 for further elaboration). It is clear from the table that there is a strong relationship between stated intention and current legal status. Those who have adjusted their visa status to that of permanent resident are far less likely to express the intention of returning to Israel than are those who still hold an educational visa. Those who take the final step of securing American citizenship are the least likely to expect to return to Israel.[3]

At about the same time as the questionnaire data were collected, the Israel Government Bureau for Professionals (IGBP) tabulated the characteristics of Israeli students who were known to have returned to Israel

Table 3.1. *Returning to Israel by legal status – a comparison of expectations with actual behavior*

A. *Expect to return to Israel by legal status among those in the study population who entered the U.S. on an educational visa (%):*		
Educational visa	66 (904)[a]	χ^2 = 354.34
Permanent resident	20 (267)	df = 2
U.S. citizen	11 (117)	$p < .001$
B. *Actually returned to Israel by legal status (%):*		
Israeli citizen	17 (1976)	χ^2 = 17.77
American or Canadian citizen	7 (275)	df = 1
		$p < .001$

[a] In this table and in all tables in this chapter, numbers in parentheses are subgroup *N*s.

and compared that group with Israelis who were still resident in the United States.[4] The IGBP made a greater effort in maintaining sojourner and returnee lists for those students who came at the graduate level, so that there is some bias built into the population lists with which they worked. However, the bias is not such as to preclude careful comparisons. The attributes for which comparisons of returnees and sojourners were made were limited to those which were part of the normal record-keeping procedure of the IGBP. The first of these is citizenship. As noted in Table 3.1, A, a smaller proportion of students with American citizenship expected to return to Israel; the IGBP data set shows that a smaller proportion of those who held American (or, in a few instances, Canadian) citizenship had actually returned to Israel (Table 3.1, B). Thus, the internal comparison and the comparison with the external data set point to the same conclusion.

The IGBP also collected data on age, marital status, and occupation–field of study, paralleling data collected by the study questionnaire. A comparison of the results of the two sets of findings is presented in Table 3.2. Again, we find that expectations and behaviors are broadly consistent. Older students are more likely to return (and expect to return) than are younger students; so, too, marriage to an Israeli predicts return; last, natural scientists are more likely to return than are engineers.

The comparisons noted in Tables 3.1 and 3.2 give reasonable warrant for concluding that the statements of intention may be taken as proxies of actual behavior *in the aggregate.* Although individual students may not fulfill their stated intentions, these "errors" are likely to cancel one another in a sufficiently large population. Panel data are the one kind of evidence that we do not have and which would permit us to make a stronger case. If, several years after collecting the information on intentions, we had collected follow-up data on actual behavior, the case would be even stronger. Given the constraints of time and money, this was not possible. Neither the American nor the Israeli government maintains continually updated files on returnees. It was beyond the scope of this study to generate such files. It should be noted, too, that, even if we had such data, we still could not be absolutely sure that in each case there was a perfect match between stated intention and actual behavior. We could note whether those who had expressed the intention of not returning had, in fact, returned and thus catch that error; that is, we could determine if students individually underestimated their propensity to return to Israel. We could not, however, be

Table 3.2. *Returning to Israel by three social attributes – a comparison of expectations with actual behavior (percentages)*

	Actually returned	Expect to return
Age at arrival:		
26 and younger	4 (421)	46 (1065)
27 and older	19 (2384)	60 (825)
	χ^2 = 56.37	χ^2 = 35.90
	df = 1	df = 1
	$p <$ .001	$p <$ .001
Marital status:		
Israeli spouse	23 (1307)	63 (917)
Single, widowed, or divorced	12 (944)	50 (450)
Non-Israeli spouse	11 (612)	29 (439)
	χ^2 = 67.04	χ^2 = 138.76
	df = 2	df = 2
	$p <$ .001	$p <$ .001
Occupation:		
Mathematics and natural sciences	25 (626)	58 (304)
Engineering	12 (894)	46 (823)
	χ^2 = 43.19	χ^2 = 11.99
	df = 1	df = 1
	$p <$ .001	$p <$ .001

sure whether students overestimated their propensity to return to Israel. Those who had expressed an intention of returning to Israel and who had still not returned to Israel at the time of the second wave of the panel study might still return at some later point.

An estimate of the magnitude of the Israeli student brain drain

If, in this particular case, statements of intention may be accepted as proxies for behavior, it does not follow that the rates of migration and repatriation in our study population can be taken at face value. The actual rate of migration among Israeli students in the United States is very probably lower than that reflected in our data.

We estimated that 51 percent of the Israeli student and alumni population *then resident* in the United States would eventually return to Israel. The key phrase is "then resident." The study population includes Israelis who were "left over" from early cohorts and whose presence in the population exaggerates the rate of brain drain. Although a brain-drain rate of 49 percent is a reasonable estimate for Israelis then resident in the United States, it exaggerates the brain-drain rate for Israeli students and alumni *ever resident* in the United States. In this section we will develop an estimate of rate of brain drain for the population ever resident in the United States. In doing so, we will take into account the effects of time in the United States on the population structure, the tendency to expect to return home, and, thus, the actual rate of brain drain among the ever resident.

The population of Israeli students in the United States is not, for the most part, permanent, but is comprised of a constant flow of persons to and from the United States. At any one time, a population count of Israeli students and former students in the United States will be biased, that is, weighted toward those who have elected to remain in the United States as immigrants. This is simply because many of those who had intended to return to Israel will have already returned; their fellows who are migrants, however, are counted in with the new student populations.

Because the study (i.e., the then resident) population thus included an ever-increasing stock of Israelis from earlier cohorts who had elected to remain in the United States, the rate of student brain drain of the ever resident population is overstated in the responses. If we start with the population of Israelis residing in the United States at the time of data collection and break it down into categories based on period of entry into the United States, the rate of "expected return" to Israel decreases as we go back in time: The rate of expectation of return to Israel *seems* to decline from 69 to 23 percent for the group who arrived in the United States in 1959 or earlier (Table 3.3, A).

By using the IGBP data set described in the foregoing, we can compute the actual rate of return by time cohorts. These data show essentially the same pattern as do the intention data from the study population. Among those who arrived two years or less before data collection, 67 percent returned home during 1966-7. Among those who arrived during 1959 or prior years, 6 percent returned during 1966-7 (Table 3.3, B). Time is associated with declining intention to return home as well as actual returning home.

Table 3.3. *Returning to Israel by period of entry into the United States – a comparison of expectations with actual behaviors*

A. *Expect to return to Israel by period of entry (%):*			
1964–6	69	(646)	$\chi^2 = 247.0$
1962–3	59	(523)	df = 3
1960–1	41	(306)	$p < .001$
1959 and prior	23	(435)	
B. *Actually returned to Israel by period of entry (%):*			
1964–6	67	(180)	$\chi^2 = 434.1$
1962–3	20	(800)	df = 3
1960–1	15	(565)	$p < .001$
1959 and prior	6	(1095)	

The key question is whether the decline in rates of intention to re-turn home manifest in the study population (and actual behavior in the IGBP population) reflects an actual decline in propensity to return or a change in the population structure. Insofar as it is the former, the brain drain rate of 49 percent is likely to be a reasonable estimate of the true figure. If it is the latter, then the 49 percent figure is likely to be an overestimate of the brain drain.

The relationship between time in the United States and intention to return home has important theoretical implications as well. Similar findings have led other investigators to infer that there is some causal relationship between time in the United States and the propensity to return for any group of foreign students.[5] However, the pattern is as likely to be artifactual as it is to be real.

For example, let us assume that, in 1964, 100 Israeli students had entered the United States, of whom 70 were sure that they would re-turn to Israel. By 1966, 30 students had returned to Israel, and these 30 were all part of the group of 70 who initially were sure that they would return. The changing stock would generate a false picture of declining intention to return. Translating this phenomenon into terms of rates of intent to return, we would find that in 1964 70 percent of the 100 Israeli students in the hypothetical sample were sure of returning, whereas by 1966 the figure is "reduced" to 57 percent of the 70 who remained.

Although the correlation between time in the United States and rate of intended (and actual) return is real, an inference of a causal relation-

Table 3.4. *1965–6 Cohort: expectation of return to Israel by time initially expected to remain in the United States*

Time initially expected to remain in the U.S.	% Expect to return to Israel	
Less than 1 year	90 (10)	χ^2 = 29.53
1–2 plus years	84 (138)	df = 4
3–4 plus years	68 (126)	$p <$ .001
5–6 plus years	66 (37)	
7 years or more	0 (6)	

ship is likely to be at least partially spurious. From the very beginning of their stay in the United States, those students who expected to remain longer in the United States in fact were more likely to have expected to remain permanently in the United States. The expectation of a long sojourn is significantly correlated with the expectation of remaining permanently. This relationship is shown in Table 3.4.

Reconstituting a hypothetical population

To be able to develop a more precise estimate of rate of return, one must, first, attempt to reconstruct the actual return flow population, going back to an earlier period in time, and, second, have a better sense of the extent to which (if any) propensity to return home declines with time in the United States. Given the population of then resident Israelis and knowledge of their intentions, we want to be able to reconstruct the population of ever resident Israelis. To do this, we shall construct a hypothetical population that will take into account the two-way flow between the United States and Israel.

The following pieces of information are available: (1) the number of Israelis in the actual study population who entered the United States by year of entry; (2) the number of student visas issued to Israelis by year of entry; (3) the rate of intention to return to Israel by year of entry. These data are used in Table 3.5 to compute the hypothetical study population and estimates of rates of actual, intended, and "total" return to Israel by year of entry into the United States.

Row A in Table 3.5 presents the number of respondents by year of entry into the United States. It shows that the number of those having

Table 3.5. *Reconstruction of total stock of Israeli students in the United States and return flows for the period 1958–65*

	'65	'64	'63	'62	'61	'60	'59	'58
A. No. of respondents (base figure)	320	326	275	248	163	143	100	89
B. No. of student visas issued	—	562	552	522	492	456	396	337
C. Index number of student visas issued (FY 1964–5 = 1.00)[a]	—	1.00	.98	.93	.88	.81	.70	.60
D. Estimate of size of reporting population assuming that all years would have had the same pattern of response	320	326	317	300	284	262	226	193
E. Estimate of the proportion of the population already returned to Israel (%)	0	0	13	17	43	45	56	54
F. Estimate of the remainder who will return presented as a percentage of the hypothetical original population	71	67	55	46	25	21	16	15
G. Estimate of the percentage of each cohort who will or have already returned	71	67	68	63	68	66	72	69
H. Estimate of the annual rate of brain drain (%)[b]	29	33	32	37	32	34	28	31

[a]FY – fiscal year.
[b]Mean annual cohort rate of return to Israel = 68%.

completed the questionnaire declines as we go back in time. Some of that decline can be attributed to the fact that the number of Israelis entering the United States has been growing steadily over the eight-year period we are examining. This increase is reflected in row B, which tallies the number of student visas issued to Israelis each year as an indicator of the total number of Israeli students who entered the United States that year. Row C gives another measure of that increase: The visas issued each year are computed as percentages of the 1964–5 figure, which is given the index number of 1.00.

But a portion of the decline in the size of the study population results from the fact that some of the students who would have answered the questionnaire have returned to Israel. We thus compute an estimate of the hypothetical reporting population for each year (row D). The hypothetical reporting population is equal to the product of the average of the reporting population for 1964 and 1965 (= 323) multiplied by the index number of student visas for the year in question. Thus, for 1962, the calculation is 323 × .93 = 300; for 1961, it is 323 × .88 = 284; and so forth. (In computing this number we have assumed a constant rate of response to the questionnaire for each year.) The difference between the hypothetical number of respondents and the actual number of respondents (row D – row A) gives us the estimate of the total number from the hypothetical population who had returned home by the time the data had been collected. The proportion who returned, expressed as a percentage of the total hypothetical population, [(row D – row A)/row D] × 100, is estimated in row E. Row E, then, is our estimated figure for rate of *actual* return, that is, the "missing" proportion of our population who, by returning to Israel, have caused it to be weighted in favor of migrants.

The estimate of the proportion of each cohort of the study population that will eventually return to Israel is derived by dividing the number in the actual study population who indicated that they would return home in each arrival cohort by the hypothetical population for each year (row D). This percentage is reported in row F. The estimate of the total percentage of each cohort who had been or would be repatriated at some time – the sum of those who did return and who expressed the intent to return – is the sum of rows E and F. This sum is presented in row G.

In examining row G, we find that there is no patterned change in rates of total return to Israel (i.e., the sum of actual and intended return) by year of entry into the United States. This is because the estimated rate of actual return (row E) and the rates of reported expected return are complementary. As we go back in time, a larger proportion of Israeli students have completed their studies and returned home – their rate of return *increases.* At the same time, the proportion of students planning to return (row F) *decreases* as a function of the return to Israel of some of their fellows who had come to the United States at the same time as they did. The relatively constant rate of total return (row G) is to be expected, given the relative constancy in structural factors underlying the migration–repatriation decisions, which is the focus of this study and the basis of the analysis in this chapter and in Chapter 5. If the assumptions made in developing this analysis are correct – and they are at least plausible – then the constant rate of total return belies the apparent "erosion" with time in intention to return to Israel, revealing it as an artifact of the population structure and not a reflection of change of mind.

Once the "leftovers" from earlier cohorts in the study population have been compensated for, the calculations in Table 3.5 generate an estimated average rate of return of 68 percent (see row H) rather than the 51 percent that would be estimated on the basis of the study population per se; that is, a rate of brain drain of 32 percent rather than 49 percent.

This rate is consistent with an estimate of the magnitude of Israeli brain drain generated by using American Immigration and Naturalization Service data. Data for student visa adjustments of Israeli students for the fiscal years 1962–4 are presented in Table 3.6.

Table **3.6.** *Number of student visas issued and number of student visas adjusted*

Student visas issued		Student visas adjusted	
Fiscal year	No.	Fiscal year	No.
1957–8	265	1961–2	71
1958–9	271	1962–3	117
1959–60	351	1963–4	73
Total	887	Total	261
Rate of adjustment = 29%			

Analysis of the study data has shown that those who adjust their status from student to permanent resident do so after being in the United States for four years on the average. Thus, for each of the years for which there were data on the adjustment of status, the number of student visas issued four years earlier was used to compute the rate of adjustment. These data and calculations show an adjustment rate of 29 percent for the three-year period – a figure that is very close to the 32 percent figure generated by the study data. We estimate, therefore, that the probable true rate of Israeli student brain drain is approximately 30 percent. In Chapter 5 we will compare Israel's brain-drain rate with that of other countries.

We now have shown that stated intentions can be taken seriously as indicators or proxies of actual behavior. Further, we have developed an estimate of the magnitude of the brain drain which is consistent with a reliable external source. In the process of performing the latter task, we have found that there is good reason to believe that Israeli student intention is not significantly affected by time in the United States. This finding is consistent with the proposition stated in the introductory chapter in which it was argued that home country factors were critical in determining both who would "drain" and the rate of drain. Now we turn to an analysis that will focus on home country conditions as determinants of migration. The central theme in the discussion will be the relationship between education and the economy and its impact on decisions made by employers in Israel and by Israeli students in the United States, resulting in the migration of some and the repatriation of others.

Differential migration as a function of educational achievement

Education and society in Israel

During the mandatory (i.e., pre-1948) period, the level of education of the Jewish community in Palestine (the *yishuv*) was more advanced than could be used effectively by the economy. Even during periods of prosperity there was underemployment; a significant portion of the labor force worked at jobs that required much less of them than they were qualified to do. The technological level was considerably lower than might be expected of an economy in which about 10 percent of the labor force consisted of university graduates and another third of graduates of secondary schools. One of the consequences of the technological deficit and the surplus of skills was an egalitarian wage structure. The highly educated workers in the labor force were employed at jobs considerably below their levels of qualification; they were paid at levels commensurate with their work, not their education.[6]

The educational level of the Jewish community of mandatory Palestine reflected the structural position and cultural traditions of European Jewry, but the economy was somewhere between that of industrialized Europe and the subsistence economies of the Levant. The Zionist movement in the Diaspora was particularly strong among students who brought their European *gymnasium* and university training with them to Palestine. The ideology of the socialist Zionists was such that many students and intellectuals looked forward to becoming proletarians, and the social realities facilitated their downward mobility. The solidly burgher German migration of the 1930s was another major source of professional and technical manpower during this period.

Although there was an infusion of capital into mandatory Palestine, much of the flow was in the form of unilateral transfers to and through the various Jewish quasi-public bodies, of which approximately 40 percent (during the period 1917–39) went for purchases of land. Relatively little money remained for the purchase of the capital equipment necessary to develop an industrial economy that, in turn, would have created demand for high-level manpower.[7]

Even the private sector, in which one would have expected the primacy of profit considerations and economic rationality, was harnessed to *national political* goals. The owners and managers of citrus groves (the major private investment in this period) were pressed to hire Jewish laborers, though they were more expensive, so that jobs could be created and thus encourage Jewish migration into the country. One of the chief catch phrases of the 1920s and 1930s was *avodah ivrit* ("Hebrew labor"). Jewish entrepreneurs were expected to hire Jewish workers rather than the cheaper (and often more efficient) Arab workers. The Histadrut, the major labor union in the country, restricted membership to Jewish workers. Its commitment to the "class struggle" was subordinated to national political goals.[8]

The leadership of the *yishuv* had little interest in industrialization. Economic, technical and professional functions were subordinated to ideological and political goals, a phenomenon characteristic of revolutionary societies. In those activities which were controlled by the national institutions (e.g., education), technical competence was less demanded (and rewarded) than was ideological purity and organizational loyalty.[9] Professionalism was seen (correctly) as a rival faith which might weaken one's commitment to the national ideal and its organizational apparatus. The establishment of the State in 1948 set off a series of events that radically changed the relationship between supply and demand for capital and labor, and altered the normative orientation of the society.

From 1948 to 1964, the Jewish population of Israel trebled, largely as a consequence of immigration. In 1948, approximately 20 percent of the population was Levantine and North African; by 1964, it was 57 percent Levantine and North African. The non-European migration had less schooling and fewer skills[10]; few were committed to Zionist or socialist ideals. At the same time that Israel was receiving a relatively uneducated population, there was a massive flow of capital into the country. From 1950 through 1962, the capital stock per worker (net of public service and dwellings) grew at the rate of 7.8 percent per annum, a growth rate far greater than that of the major industrial powers.[11] The situation became the reverse of that which obtained during the mandatory period: Israel became (relatively) rich in physical resources and poor in human resources. The demand for professional manpower began to reflect itself in growing income differentials, with education becoming a more powerful determinant of income as skill became scarce and its price rose. The egalitarian ethic of the mandatory period was being chipped away by the economic necessities of a dynamic industrializing economy. The demand for high-level manpower absorbed the skill surplus and began to grow more rapidly than the available supply.

Supply and demand for high-level manpower

Although Israeli higher education antedates the establishment of the state by a generation, the university system in the prestate period consisted of two small institutions, the Technion (Israel Institute of Technology in Haifa) and the Hebrew University in Jerusalem. During the first twenty-five years of its history, the Hebrew University conferred only 876 degrees, about thirty-five graduates per year. By and large, the emphasis at the Hebrew University was on the theoretical disciplines. The law faculty was not established until 1948, and the medical faculty in 1949.[12] The professional manpower needs were largely met by immigration. With the establishment of the state, the university system grew enormously, but that growth was uneven and insufficient for meeting local manpower needs. From 1962 to 1966, the total number of students enrolled in Israeli universities almost doubled, whereas the number of doctoral candidates increased only by about one-sixth.[13] (Although the pattern has since changed, with a more rapid expansion in graduate than undergraduate education, it prevailed at the time of the study.) Most of the growth occurred in the traditional (and inexpensive) nonlaboratory fields, with an ever-decreasing ratio of students enrolled in science and technology.[14] Even had the economy been growing at a much slower rate, Israel would still have been dependent on foreign sources for some of its skilled manpower. In some fields (e.g., veterinary medicine), the few new professionals needed each year made it impractical and uneconomical for a small country to establish training facilities at home.

The continuing shortage of high-level manpower made it desirable and even necessary for some employers to depend on foreign sources to train some of their manpower. Many of these employers make job commitments to students before they go abroad, in order to insure themselves of an adequate supply of skilled personnel. When the student goes abroad with the assurance of a job, he has a great advantage over his colleagues who must take their chances in the Israeli labor market when (and if) they return home. Many students abroad are not at all sure that the skills that they have labored after are, in fact, in demand at home. Years of study may turn out to have been invested unwisely, at least in terms of the occupational opportunity structure in Israel. The student who is assured of a job need not worry. Rather than his taking a risk in returning home, the prospective employer underwrites the risk by assuming it himself. Thus, among those in the study population, whereas only 46 percent without job commitments expected to return home, 79 percent of those with such commitments expected to go back.[15]

The assurance of a job for a student going abroad gives him an advantaged position in the Israeli opportunity structure, which is reflected in the higher rate of repatriation of those students. His advantage is gained through the willingness of an employer to entertain certain costs and risks. Rather than wait for a student to return home, the employer could hire a foreign expert, although this alternative tends to be very expensive. Another possibility would be to go into the local labor market and outbid his competitors for certain classes of highly trained and skilled professionals. This alternative is employed, but it too has its limitations. First, the special skills he needs might not exist in Israel at all, or might not be available locally in sufficient quantity to meet his needs. Second, if he were to outbid competitors significantly, to pay the salaries necessary to recruit the men he requires, he would upset the entire wage structure of his enterprise and would tend to generate demand for higher wages among other employees. It is to the advantage of some employers to make job commitments in advance, despite the opportunity costs and risks involved.

Employers who are dependent on foreign training require evidence that a prospective employee is the right person for the job. This is the case even where the employer is hiring for immediate employment and where there is an open and free labor market. It is even more so in the situation under discussion where the normal risks of employment are increased by its being delayed and by the peculiar structure of employment tenure that obtains in Israel. Workers at every level, from the simple common laborer to the most sophisticated professional and managerial personnel, are protected by both formal and informal rules of tenure. It is extremely difficult to dismiss a worker once he has been hired unless the employer is able to show just cause, and in such cases he must pay rather large compensation sums to the employee who has been dismissed. Under these conditions, the Israeli employer is constrained even more than his American counterpart to be prudent in hiring workers.

The best evidence of future accomplishment is past accomplishment. The better the student's school record and the more professional experience he has had, the more likely he is to report a job commitment from an employer. The measure of academic achievement in Israel takes into account both the highest degree earned in Israel and undergraduate grade-point average for those who completed their Bachelor's in Israel. The effect of educational achievement is not restricted to credentialing, as expressed in diplomas, certificates, and degrees. Equally important as a determinant of the student's opportunities is the *quality* of his work in school: Forty percent of those with a high average (i.e., with the equivalent of B or better, irrespective of degree level) have job assurances, as compared with only 22 percent of those with low grade-point averages. The meritocratic standards that regulate access to higher levels

Table 3.7. *Report of a job commitment in Israel by academic achievement in Israel and by work in field in Israel*

	% Reporting a job commitment in Israel	
A. *Report of job commitment in Israel by academic achievement in Israel (highest degree and grades):*		
No degree from Israel	10 (1257)	χ^2 = 183.90
Bachelor's		
Low grades	16 (273)	df = 4
High grades	24 (90)	p < .001
Graduate		
Low grades	31 (166)	
High grades	49 (148)	
B. *Report of a job commitment in Israel by work in field in Israel:*		
Did not work in field	6 (983)	χ^2 = 143.25
Worked in field	26 (951)	df = 1
		p < .001

of the Israeli educational system also have application within the occupational system (Table 3.7).[16]

The effects of educational achievement and professional experience cannot be fully separated. The timing of the student's trip abroad depends on his educational achievement. The weaker his academic achievement, the less opportunity he has had to acquire professional experience. Academic achievement "causes" professional experience. However, from the employer's perspective, both predictors of future accomplishment are presented simultaneously. When professional experience in Israel has been a factor in securing a job commitment, the job is usually held open by an employer for whom he has worked. The usual sequence of events is that the student has worked in his field in Israel, receives an unpaid leave, and has his employer's assurance that his job is being held open for him.[17] The employer's decision is based at least in part on his *own* experience with the worker, rather than on references from a prior employer. The entire process operates within the relatively narrow confines of a given firm or organization.

Table 3.8. *Report of a job commitment in
Israel by Israeli high school matriculation
examination grades among those who
completed high school in Israel*

Grades earned	%Reporting a job commitment in Israel	
No examination	10 (227)	$\chi^2 = 19.38$
		df = 4
6–6.5	13 (123)	$p < .001$
7–7.5	13 (499)	
8–8.5	20 (483)	
9–9.5	23 (102)	

When an employer uses academic achievement as his hiring criterion, he is inferring future achievement in one institutional area or role from past achievement in another area or role. He is, in effect, depending on the school system to screen prospective employees and is accepting judgments made by academic authorities as to the probable value of his prospective employee. As reported in Chapter 2, performance in high school controls access to the universities in Israel and is a reasonable predictor of academic performance in the university. It follows that high school academic achievement might indirectly predict whether or not a student has a job waiting for him in Israel (Table 3.8).

Alternative opportunity structures

Although Israeli students grant the importance of ability and academic achievement in getting ahead in Israel, many tend to see an inordinately significant role played by political and familial ties, particularly as compared with the United States. For example, only 50 percent of these students felt that ability is very important in advancing one's career in Israel as compared with 76 percent who felt that ability was very important in the United States; 20 percent thought that family connections were very important in Israel as compared with only 6 percent who believed this about the United States; 28 percent felt that political connections were very important in Israel as compared with only 3 percent who felt they were important in the United States.

There is much in Israel to make these students believe that particularistic ties are significant in advancing their careers. By virtue of being a small society, many Israelis have access to high-level government officials to whom they are related or with whom they went to school or served in the army or with whom they grew up in the "old country." By virtue of Israel's being a new society, the social stratification system is still fluid so that access to persons in high places is relatively common. Most of the population of Israel is not far removed from the traditional societies of Eastern Europe and the Levant, in which particularistic considerations were a significant part of everyday life. The economy itself is highly politicized, giving rise to the appearance and, in some instances, the reality that government loans and other forms of government intervention in the economy are based at least in part on political loyalties and connections.

One alternative to achievement-based recruitment was suggested in the previous chapter. It was shown that social class of origin was a significant factor in gaining access to educational opportunity. The lower the student's social origins, the less likely was he to have earned a degree in Israel before coming to the United States, and the more likely was he to have been a Second Chancer. Social class operated most powerfully in the move from primary school to high school, in that those who came from lower-class homes were less likely to have attended academic high schools. However, if students successfully entered academic high schools, their social origins played a much smaller role in determining their academic achievement.

Because academic achievement is so closely linked with opportunity in Israel, what, if any, *direct* effect does social class have on opportunity and, in turn, on migration? The correlation between social class origin and job commitment in Israel is .04 and is reduced to .02 when controlled for academic achievement and professional experience in Israel. The correlation between social class origin and expectation of return to Israel is .05 and is reduced to .03 when controlled for academic achievement, professional experience in Israel, and job commitment in Israel.[18] These correlations (both zero-order and partials) are much lower than that which obtains between social class origin and academic achievement in Israel ($R = .13$). Although social class is an important predictor of entrance into the university track within the

Table **3.9**. *Report of a job commitment in Israel and expectation of return to Israel by social class origin (percentages)*

Social class origin as measured by father's highest level of education	Job com- mitment in Israel	Expectation of return to Israel
Primary school	14 (588)	48 (588)
High school	17 (777)	52 (777)
College or university	18 (569)	53 (569)
	$\chi^2 = 3.75$	$\chi^2 = 3.46$
	df = 2	df = 2
	$p < .2$	$p < .2$

secondary school system, it has little effect beyond that. The critical problem for lower-class Israelis is that of entering the university track at the secondary school level. If they manage to do this their initial ascriptive disadvantage largely disappears (Table 3.9).

In their comments about the relative significance of personal influence and achievement in furthering a career, the students seemed to be expressing an overly roseate view of American society and a jaundiced view of their own country. Studies of American society suggest that a significant proportion of Americans believe in the power of influence in American society. Americans call special influence "pull" or "drag"; Israelis call it *proteksia*.[19] Irrespective of label, it is the same phenomenon. Every country probably has a word for it. Just to what extent *proteksia* is significant in accounting for access to opportunities among various countries and just where it is helpful is only dimly known. One would expect that the use of a *proteksia* system would be characteristic of (and more legitimate in) traditional, less developed societies.

There is no doubt that the *proteksia* system operates in Israel. There is little doubt that it is effective in many areas of everyday life in Israel. It is probably the ubiquitous character of petty *proteksia* that moves some of the Israeli students to believe that professional careers in Israel can be helped by *proteksia*. It is precisely those students who are academically weak and/or do not have job experience in Israel who are most likely to claim *proteksia* ties which they believe will be useful in furthering their careers in Israel (Table 3.10, A and B). There is also a

Table 3.10. *Claim of* proteksia *by academic achievement in Israel and by work in field in Israel and by report of a job commitment in Israel*

	% Claiming proteksia	
A. *Claim of* proteksia *by academic achievement in Israel (highest degree and grades):*		
No degree from Israel	37 (1257)	χ^2 = 89.40
Bachelor's		df = 4
Low grades	28 (273)	p < .001
High grades	11 (90)	
Graduate		
Low grades	15 (166)	
High grades	10 (148)	
B. *Claim of* proteksia *by work in field in Israel:*	36 (983)	χ^2 = 26.95
Did not work in field	25 (951)	df = 1
Worked in field		p < .001
C. *Correlations between claim of* proteksia *and report of a job commitment in Israel:*		
Zero-order correlation	–.125	
Partial correlation controlling for academic achievement in Israel and work in field in Israel	–.055	

negative relationship between claiming *proteksia* and the existence of a job commitment in Israel, suggesting initially that students who are unsuccessful in securing a job commitment invoke *proteksia* and/or that professionally inexperienced, academically weaker students unsuccessfully invoke *proteksia.* The causal direction cannot be determined. However, because both variables, claiming *proteksia* and job commitment in Israel, are functions of the two prior variables and the relationship is significantly reduced when controlled for academic achievement and professional experience in Israel, we may conclude that the relationship is largely causally spurious (Table 3.10, C)

A more plausible interpretation, then, is that everyone has some *proteksia* ties, but that the willingness to admit to them and try or plan to use them at this level is more common among those students whose advancement on the basis of achievement is more problematic. High achievers, both academic and professional, seem more content to attempt to pursue their careers in Israel through the achievement-oriented opportunity structure. In the case of lower achievement, the student is both more likely to invoke other possible avenues to occupational success and to be prepared to use, even though unsuccessfully, what are, in fact, deviant avenues to professional advancement in Israel.[20]

The professional opportunity structure in Israel is based on achievement rather than *proteksia*; yet the fear of the power of the *proteksia* system continues and seems to affect the behavior of some students. Over 28 percent of the respondents indicated that the existence of the *proteksia* system in Israel might be a reason for remaining permanently in the United States, and those who expressed fear of the *proteksia* system were, in fact, less likely to expect to return to Israel (Table 3.11). There is no way of being certain whether their expressed fear of the *proteksia* system actually motivated their decision not to return home or was an after-the-fact rationalization. Significantly, however, in a list of possible reasons for not returning home, expressed fear of the *proteksia* system was the "rationalization of choice" among weaker students, who have not had professional experience in Israel and who have no job commitments (Table 3.12). Having done less well in Israel, they misattributed their relative failure to some characteristic of the Israeli society. At the very least, their expressed fear of the *proteksia* system offered a plausible reason for not returning to Israel; yet, as we have seen, the available evidence suggests that the *proteksia* system as a means of securing *professional* employment is largely inoperative and mythical. Belief in the reality of *proteksia* leads to a situation in which

Table 3.11. *Expectation of return to Israel by expression of fear of* proteksia *system in Israel*

	% Expecting to return to Israel	
Expresses fear of *proteksia* system	35 (550)	χ^2 = 81.93
Does not express fear of *proteksia* system	58 (1384)	df = 1
		$p < .001$

Table 3.12. *Expression of fear of* proteksia *system in Israel by academic achievement in Israel and by job commitment in Israel*

	% Expressing fear of *proteksia* system	
A. *Fear of* proteksia *system by academic achievement in Israel (highest degree and grades):*		
No degree from Israel	33 (1257)	χ^2 = 43.59
Bachelor's		df = 4
Low grades	23 (273)	p < .001
High grades	20 (90)	
Graduate		
Low grades	18 (166)	
High grades	14 (148)	
B. *Fear of* proteksia *system by job commitment in Israel:*		
Does not report a job commitment	31 (1621)	χ^2 = 31.69
Reports a job commitment	15 (313)	df = 1
		p < .001

relative failure in the Israeli academic and occupational systems breeds a form of self-serving alienation from Israel. The corollary of this proposition is that the better students are more likely to believe in the meritocratic character of the opportunity structure in Israel and are more likely to have faith in their own ability to get on in Israel, based on their own achievements.

We have pointed to a set of five interrelated variables or factors that may be understood as operating as a system: academic achievement, prior work experience in Israel, a job commitment in Israel, fear of *proteksia,* and intent to return. These variables link Israel's schools to the economy and ultimately to the students' migration intentions.

Path model for analyzing Israeli student migration intentions

To understand and summarize how they work as a system, we have presented a path model in Figure 3.1. The model permits us to take

CORRELATION MATRIX

	X_1	X_2	X_3	X_4	X_5
X_1 Academic achievement	×				
X_2 Worked in Israel	.301	×			
X_3 Job in Israel	.308	.270	×		
X_4 Fear of *proteksia*	−.146	−.104	−.128	×	
X_5 Expect to return	.212	.104	.274	−.224	×

PATH MODEL

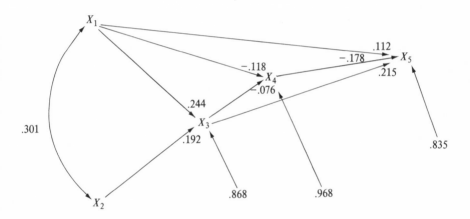

Figure 3.1 Basic path analytic model of Israeli student migration intentions. (Full sample, N = 1,934.)

into account all of the relevant factors simultaneously and to examine the relationships among the variables. The path model will be used as a summary statement of the linkages and microtheories presented in the earlier parts of this chapter. We will build on the bivariate relations developed earlier in the chapter.

In developing a path model, there are two essential tasks to perform. First, we must order the variables in a way that reveals a causal structure making good theoretical sense. Second, we must estimate the effects of the independent variables on the dependent variables. Specifying a causal order with cross-sectional data is always a somewhat problematic enterprise. Where temporal order is ostensibly clear (e.g., parent's education and child's education), the problem is solved by the apparently self-evident priority of one variable with respect to another. Here the problem is more complex but not completely insoluble. We shall make explicit the implicit ordering presented in the tables earlier in this chapter.

The two primary facts about each of the students are their academic achievement and professional experience in Israel. These are the exogenous variables upon which the system is built. The argument presented earlier in the chapter was that potential employers used the criteria of achievement and experience in deciding whether to assume the risk of making a job commitment to the student before his return. The three variables – academic achievement, work in field in Israel, and job commitment in Israel – together reflected the Israeli professional opportunity structure and the student's probability of success within that structure. We further found that some students expressed the fear that the Israeli opportunity structure was built on personal and political connections, namely *proteksia,* and claimed this fear would keep them from returning. For this analysis, we accept at face value their word (even though somewhat gingerly) that fear of *proteksia* in fact motivated their decision and was not an after-the-fact rationalization.

Finally, we come to the ultimate dependent variable, the intent to return to Israel or remain in the United States. This we take as the final fact in the causal chain. It might be argued that those who initially expected to return to Israel prudently secured jobs for themselves prior to coming to the United States to study and, thus, that the intention to return is temporally prior to a job commitment. This argument, though plausible, faces two problems. First, why should employers make those job commitments without taking into account their own interests? Assuming that the employers' own needs would call for their making these commitments to the best people around, it seems reasonable to conclude that they exercised such judgment before committing themselves, in line with the pattern suggested here. Second, we found that the existence of a job commitment in Israel was either uncorrelated or very weakly correlated with several measures of personal preference to return or subjective commitment to Israel, either ideological or sentimental. The student does not have a job waiting for him as a result primarily of his personal preference: The job awaits him as a consequence of some employer's need for his services and evidence of his own probable competence.

Having specified a causal structure, we return to the covariation among the variables and attempt to estimate the direct and indirect effects of each of the independent variables on the three dependent variables. To simplify the model and eliminate substantively trivial effects, direct paths are noted in those instances in which the unstandardized regression coefficient is at least three times the size of its standard error. This relatively large multiple is used because of the large sample size, which tends to report small, and possibly substantively trivial, relationships as statistically significant.

First it is shown that the direct effects of academic achievement (X_1) and work in field in Israel (X_2) on job commitment in Israel (X_3) are slightly smaller than their respective correlations. This is a function of the correlation between the two independent variables. Thus,

$$r_{31} = p_{31} + p_{32}\, r_{12} \quad \text{and} \quad r_{32} = p_{32} + p_{31}\, r_{12}$$

The relationship between X_1 and X_3 is composed of the direct effect of X_1 on X_3 and the indirect effect which is traced through the correlation of X_1 and X_2 multiplied by the direct effect of X_2 on X_3.

By solving the pair of simultaneous equations, we have the formula for computing path coefficients:

$$p_{31} = \frac{r_{31} - r_{32}\, r_{12}}{1 - r_{12}^{\,2}} \qquad p_{32} = \frac{r_{32} - r_{31}\, r_{12}}{1 - r_{12}^{\,2}}$$

Variables X_1, X_2, and X_3 are then examined for possible direct effects on X_4. By proceeding with the same logic presented in the three-variable case (although the computation is somewhat more complex), we find that there is a direct effect of X_1 and X_3 on X_4, but that X_2 has no direct effect on X_4. That is, although those who worked in field in Israel (X_2) are less likely to express fear of *proteksia* (X_4), the relationship should not be construed as directly causal. Rather, the lack of fear of *proteksia* is *directly* caused by the students' having actual job commitments (X_3) and, prior to that, high academic achievement (X_1). It is not knowledge of the system, based on work experience, which makes the difference in one's perceptions and fears of the system. Rather it is the confidence engendered by achievement and an assurance of a job.

Direct effects on migration intent are noted from academic achievement (X_1), job commitment in Israel (X_3), and fear of *proteksia* (X_4). There is no *direct* effect of work in field in Israel (X_2). Thus work experience in Israel in and of itself does not encourage the student's plan for return home: It has to be mediated by confidence in the system (i.e., the absence of the fear of *proteksia*) and, even more, by a job commitment from an employer in Israel. By contrast, academic achievement does have a *direct* effect on migration intent in addition to its indirect effect operating through the two intervening variables of job commitment and fear of *proteksia*. A little more than half the total effect of academic achievement remains as a direct effect; that is, the better the student, the more likely is he to plan to return home because (1) he has a job waiting for him, (2) he is not afraid of *proteksia*, and (3) he is a good student. As a good student he probably has confidence in his ability to "make it" in Israel. The evidence presented here suggests that his confidence is warranted.

Academic achievement, then, is the key variable in the system, significantly correlated with, and a direct cause of, the other variables. It influences employers' decisions to offer jobs, students' perceptions of the equity of the opportunity structure, and migration intent itself. The school system, then, in addition to its primary functions of socialization and education, has played a critical role in the allocation of opportunity and ultimately the propensity to migrate or return home among those Israelis who continue their education abroad. In the next sections of this chapter, we will test this model of a universalistic, achievement-oriented opportunity structure, and then extend the analysis to an examination of its operation in particular economic sectors of Israeli society.

Personal influence and instrumental need

The thesis underlying this discussion has been that the demand for manpower – and the student's response to that demand – can be fully understood largely in terms of objective market and social structural forces. If Israel were not short of high-level manpower, employers would not feel constrained to entertain the costs involved in making long-term job commitments. The students, in turn, respond to the opportunity structure in terms of their own need to secure their future. The opportunity structure worked to induce the best Israeli students to return home, not as a consequence of central planning or patriotic sentiment, but as a result of each actor in the system acting independently to maximize his individual utility without reference to societal considerations. The key variables operative in that system were the *objective* attributes of the students and the employers. We assumed that the various actors in the system were motivated by self-interest; the burden of the analysis was that of determining the nature and location of that self-interest and its consequences for the process of repatriation.

When personal loyalties were introduced into the model in the form of claims of *proteksia,* we found that the consequences were nil or even the reverse of those intended. The reason for the power of the market model is that the employer–employee relationship is a classic case of economic rationality. Although personal loyalties may and do develop between employers and employees, both parties are constrained to act in conformity with forces that are external both to their relationship and perhaps even to their personal preferences. Their relationship is reducible to mutual self-interest.

The relationship between the student and his professors in Israel has much of a market character as well. Academic achievement has its reward in occupational opportunity. The higher educational system and the economy are closely linked to one another, and on some levels there is little to distinguish the situation of students and workers. Both are evaluated universalistically in terms of performance (however measured) rather than particularistically in terms of personal qualities. Relationships in universities are significantly determined by the student's intellectual achievements. The student is oriented toward his professor in terms of the professor's ability to help him advance his career. The professor sees him as a junior colleague. Sentiment plays a small role in determining the character of faculty–student relationships. The higher the level of education, the higher the quality of education, the more likely it is that faculty–student ties would be governed by instrumental considerations not significantly different from those which govern employer–employee relationships within the economy. Moral and sentimental ties have been extruded as higher education has forgone character development and socialization and has focused almost exclusively on training for intellectual and vocational competence. Thus, one would expect little or no difference between the behavior and attitudes of professors and employers. The corollary of this proposition is that there would be little to distinguish the response of students to prospective employers and to former professors.

These propositions are represented concretely in the kind of advice that students report receiving and their response to that advice. All Israeli sources, insofar as they give any advice at all, tend to advise students to return home.[21] However, the advice of former professors and prospective employers is conditioned by the same set of factors that accounts for the student's being assured of a job and his intent to return to Israel. Academic achievement, professional experience, and job commitment predict the student's receiving advice from Israeli faculty and employers to return to Israel (Table 3.13). As citizens, both professors and employers might wish that all Israeli students would return home, but they work actively at repatriating only those whose return would make sense in terms of narrower occupational or economic interests (Table 3.13).

The students are aware of the instrumental character of their relationship with employers and professors. Although there is a correlation between receiving such advice and their expectation of returning (Table 3.14), it is not because the advice is heeded, but rather that the student's position in the instrumental complex motivates his plans. The student's interest in prospective employers and former professors is in terms of their ability to deliver (i.e., to help the student further his career in Israel), which, in turn, is a function of his own academic and professional achievement. The professorial and employer advice in and of itself is without consequence, as Table 3.14 demonstrates.

Sectoral variations in the basic model

The drive toward rationalization and professionalism that underlies the aggregate opportunity structure has not been equally characteristic of all sectors of Israeli society. On the whole we may see the reward of school and job achievement in terms of objective needs, and a manpower shortage requiring job commitments that, in turn, demand the development of criteria for making such commitments. Yet there are sectoral variations in basic institutional characteristics that are reflected in variations in sectoral opportunity structures, implying in turn: (1) self-selection among students, making for an initial matching of employee characteristics and institutional needs; (2) differential demand for high-level manpower by sector; (3) variation in criteria of selecting manpower by sector. Insofar as migration propensities reflect the Israeli opportunity structure, the several sectors should vary both in the kinds of students they repatriate and in the rates of repatriation by sector.

Table 3.13. *Advice from Israeli professors and employers by academic achievement, by work in field in Israel, and by job commitment in Israel*

	% Israeli Professors advising return to Israel	% Israeli Employers advising return to Israel
A. *Advice by academic achievement in Israel (highest degree and grades):*		
No degree from Israel	11 (1257)	15 (1257)
Bachelor's		
Low grades	15 (273)	23 (273)
High grades	27 (90)	32 (90)
Graduate		
Low grades	31 (166)	32 (166)
High grades	36 (148)	43 (148)
	$\chi^2 = 110.35$	$\chi^2 = 91.73$
	df = 4	df = 4
	$p < .001$	$p < .001$
B. *Advice by work in field in Israel:*		
Did not work in field	12 (983)	11 (983)
Worked in field	21 (951)	29 (951)
	$\chi^2 = 21.2$	$\chi^2 = 97.67$
	df = 1	df = 1
	$p < .001$	$p < .001$
C. *Advice by job commitment in Israel:*		
Does not report job commitment	14 (1621)	14 (1621)
Reports job commitment	31 (313)	54 (313)
	$\chi^2 = 54.4$	$\chi^2 = 255.2$
	df = 1	df = 1
	$p < .001$	$p < .001$

In order to examine the variation in opportunity and its implications for migration, we will examine three sectors of Israeli society in detail: universities, private industry, and government. Each of these sectors has a distinct history, contemporary structure, and need for high-level manpower. We will attempt to show how the characteristics of the sector influence its opportunity structure and the migration patterns of its

Table 3.14. *Expectation to return to Israel by advice from professors and employers in Israel*

	% Expecting to return to Israel	
A. *Expectation to return by advice from professors in Israel:*		
To return to Israel	61 (315)	χ^2 = 15.96
No advice reported	50 (1572)	df = 2
To remain in the U.S.	39 (47)	$p < .001$
B. *Expectation to return by advice from employers in Israel:*		
To return to Israel	63 (391)	χ^2 = 30.92
No advice reported	48 (1515)	df = 2
To remain in the U.S.	48 (28)	$p < .001$
C. *Correlations between expectation to return to Israel and advice from professors and employers in Israel:*		Partial correlation controlling for academic achievement and job commitment in Israel
	Zero-order correlation	
Expectation to return and professors' advice	.09	.03
Expectation to return and employers' advice	.12	.01

constituents.[22] After briefly reviewing the relevant characteristics of each sector, we shall then compare them with one another and with the aggregate model.

Universities. It is widely accepted that Israeli universities are of generally superior quality, demanding high levels of performance from faculty and students alike. An observer from the American National Science Foundation commented that academic ". . . science in Israel is of higher quality and better developed than in any country in Western Europe, with the possible exception of Great Britain and Sweden."[23] Other commentators have also noted the high level of pure (as opposed to applied) research in Israel.[24] Various objective indicators also point to high academic quality. Israeli academic science is heavily funded by nonpolitical, extramural sources; Israeli scholars are significant contributors to academic journals; Israeli scholars spend a good part of their leave time at prestigious American and European institutions and serve as hosts to large numbers of foreign scholars.

Even during the prestate period when the national institutions were dominated by political parties, the Technion and the Hebrew University were largely independent of political influence, a tradition that is still maintained. Funds for higher education, which were raised through the omnibus Zionist apparatus, were segregated at the source to be applied for research and teaching. In some respects these institutions were in, but not of, the Palestinian Jewish community, maintaining their distinct identity and academic integrity.

The emphasis in these institutions has always been primarily on research rather than teaching. The Hebrew University was originally organized around research institutes that became formal instructional units many years later. Even when teaching became an important part of the university's activities, it was oriented toward the training of professional scholars and scientists rather than toward undergraduate education. The B.A. program at the Hebrew University was not organized until 1949, a quarter century after the founding of the institution.

The faculties of the Israeli institutions were composed largely of European Jews who received their training in European universities. With the destruction of the pool of Jewish scholarly and scientific talent during the Second World War and with the growth of demand for faculty personnel, it became necessary to find new sources of manpower and training. Some of this demand could be met by Israeli institutions; however, even where Israel has had the capacity to train young scholars through the doctoral level, it has been the practice in many disciplines to encourage some of the best students to study abroad. In Israel, professional specialization begins with the junior year of high school (see Chapter 2), and this early specialization has an important impact on the student's later career. It is difficult, for example, for a student who has taken his matriculation exam in the humanities or social sciences to succeed later in natural science or engineering faculties.

The student's intellectual horizon narrows as he proceeds into the university. He enrolls in a faculty (the major administrative unit in the university), and within the faculty selects departments and subdepartments. There is the danger that his intellectual perspective may become constricted by being overwhelmingly exposed to one point of view. Academic authorities, fearful of the intellectual timidity and provincialism that such a system produces, encourage students to do graduate work or postdoctoral work abroad, so that they may learn other approaches to their fields and bring them back to Israel.[25] For the universities, study abroad avoids the inbreeding, particularism, and parochialism that are a constant danger for a small isolated society. In addition, Israeli universities, which have been expanding rapidly, have required high-level manpower beyond their training capacity.

Private industry. Private industry is a late entry into the Israeli economy. During the Second World War, Palestine produced goods for the British Army and the local market as a result of being cut off from industrial sources overseas. The industrial share of the total product in the Jewish economy grew from 26 percent in 1936 to 41 percent in 1945. As one set of observers put it, ". . . the war-induced expansion marked the emergence of real manufacturing as opposed to crafts."[26]

Much of Israeli private industry still remains in the hands of those who became "industrialists" during this period. Though their enterprises have grown, their entrepreneurial orientation has remained that of the artisan and shopkeeper. Many of these Israeli firms are small, family-owned enterprises concerned with adapting to the market rather than creating markets. They have not had to be aggressive in developing product lines, since the government has protected them from international competition. They are wary of modern management techniques that would remove some control from the family and put it in the hands of technocrats. When new technologies are needed, they are more likely to be purchased from abroad rather than developed at home.[27]

The private sector's share of net domestic product, particularly in manufacturing, *declined* from 1953 to 1959.[28] The major technologically sophisticated manufacturing firms in Israel are disproportionately in the public or quasi-public sector. Petrochemicals, precision engineering, and electronics are either outright government and/or Histadrut companies or are spinoffs from government enterprises. Among the most sophisticated industries in the country are those which have grown out of Ministry of Defense operations. The largest single employer of professional engineers is Bedek, the Israel Aircraft Corporation, a government company.

Standards of performance in Israeli private industry have been set with reference to local consumer demands. Israeli private industry has operated as a hothouse plant, protected from the vicissitudes of international competition by high tariff walls. Not constrained economically to invest heavily in research and development, it has not been required to hire research personnel. Research is largely a government activity in Israel. As of the early 1960s, only 18 percent of all scientists and engineers in Israel were employed by private industry, as compared with 41 percent in the United Kingdom and 56 percent in the United States.[29] More generally, Israeli private industry is not a major employer of high-level manpower because of its low level of technology. It needs relatively few professionals and those it needs usually do not require advanced training in science and technology.

Government. The governance of mandatory Palestine was uneasily shared by the British colonial office and the Jewish quasi-voluntaristic institutions.[30] Few Jews worked in the British civil service. After a relatively brief honeymoon period, the British officials were seen as unsympathetic to Jewish national aspirations. A Jew who worked for the British was necessarily suspect in regard to his loyalties to the *yishuv.* Once the mandate ended and an indigenous civil service was required, those Jews who had been members of the British civil service and who wished to continue their work under the new government of the State of Israel were closely examined for their loyalty to the state.

During the mandatory period, the major Jewish "civil service" employment was in the Jewish national institutions and the political parties. National loyalty was mediated by the parties, which, in turn, vied for control of the Jewish Agency, the Vaad Leumi (The National Committee), and the Histadrut (The Workers Federation). Within these national bodies, appointments were made on grounds of loyalty, which led to what was called the "key" system. Each party had a quota of jobs in the Jewish civil service. The nature of the prestate Jewish bureaucracy has been characterized as follows: "The absence of administrative traditions on the one hand, and the spirit of pioneering devotion on the other, together with the party 'key,' are the outstanding characteristics of the staffs of the Jewish Agency and the Vaad Leumi."[31]

It was through party discipline that the higher levels of officialdom could maintain control over the national institutions. In turn, the power to make appointments (and thus supply a livelihood) became a powerful instrument in maintaining party loyalty. Thus, the parties and the national bureaucracy were mutually reinforcing. With the establishment of the state, no less than seventeen ministries were created. The number did not reflect especially difficult problems of administering the State of Israel, but rather the interests of the parties in maintaining the "key" system as an instrument in furthering and securing party power.

The withdrawal of the British mandate created an administrative vacuum which was only partially filled by local resources. The administrative staffs, who were moved from the Jewish national apparatus to the state bureaucracy, had been developed under a set of conditions that were rapidly being phased out. One of the major problems facing the infant state was that of rationalizing government structure and the delivery of public services. Rationalization in this instance meant the development of uniform standards of performance throughout the public sector; employment based on competence rather than party loyalty; creation of an attractive, coherent career line within government service. The new conditions generated by statehood created a demand for highly trained manpower whose primary loyalty was to the state rather than to the party, to sectarian ideology, or even to a specific government or minister. As the process of rationalization continued, the demand for manpower grew.

As much as the British were distrusted and disliked, there was admiration for their professionalism and sangfroid. Critics of the low estate of government service in the early years of the state invoked the British civil service as the standard of comparison. Various aspects of British procedure were emulated, at least ritually if not substantively. In the early 1950s the government began to issue public tenders and established examinations for the higher grades in government service (although these procedures were often set aside); a civil service commission was established in 1954 with the burden of regulating and overseeing government service. In 1956 and again in 1961, laws were enacted that restricted the partisan political activities of government workers.

The change from political considerations to employment by competence (in part as certified by academic record) has had two functions and perhaps two motives. First, the demand for technically competent manpower has grown apace with the demand for technical services made on the government. The technical services that had been supplied externally by the British had to be supplied by the indigenous government once the state was founded. Second, in order to shift loyalties from the parties to the central government, the government had to reduce the power of the parties. One way of doing this was to establish criteria for government employment that would not lend themselves to party control or manipulation.

The evidence available suggests that the rationalization of the civil service has been successful. A recent study of the highest grade in the Israeli civil service (grade 19) found that 50 percent of the incumbents of this position held university degrees; of these, one-third held graduate degrees; of these, half held doctorates. An analysis of the occupational mobility patterns of these top civil servants also shows that party activity did not make for more rapid advancement in the civil service, but higher education did. By the 1960s, government service, once the preserve of ideologues and party activists, had become an attractive professional career line for young, university-trained technocrats.[32]

Effects of sectoral characteristics on opportunity structure and migration plans

On the basis of these differences, we can anticipate different situations and intentions on the part of students planning to work in the various sectors. We can expect the private sector, with the least technical sophistication, to have the weakest demand for high-level manpower, be least constrained to use academic criteria in choosing its workers, and be far the least likely to make job commitments to students going abroad. By contrast, both universities and government, needing high-level manpower, will make greater commitments of funds and jobs.

In Table 3.15, we have disaggregated the study population in terms of the sectors of expected employment. We can thus examine the impact of these sectors on the opportunity structures and hence the migration intentions of members of the study population. Through self-selection, each sector "recruits" the pool of potential workers most appropriate for the sector. In our study, the educational level of those who expected to work for private industry was much below those who expected to work in universities or government. Private sector workers

Table 3.15. *Characteristics of students by sector of expected employ-ment (percentages)*

Characteristics	Private industry	University	Govern-ment	
Bachelor's or beyond	24 (218)	60 (165)	43 (61)	χ^2 = 51.41 df = 2 $p < .001$
High grades earned by those with Bachelor's	25 (53)	36 (99)	39 (26)	χ^2 = 2.57 df = 2 $p < .3$
Worked in field in Israel	43 (218)	62 (165)	69 (61)	χ^2 = 19.82 df = 2 $p < .001$
Job commitment in Israel	6 (218)	44 (165)	51 (61)	χ^2 = 92.72 df = 2 $p < .001$
Expect to return home	29 (218)	56 (165)	74 (61)	χ^2 = 50.94 df = 2 $p < .001$

were less likely to have worked in their fields in Israel and were most likely to express fear of *proteksia*. They were also the group least likely to expect to return to Israel (Table 3.15).

Thus, the differences between the sectors do produce significantly different opportunity structures and patterns and rates of repatriation. These patterns and structures are shown in Table 3.16 where we repli-cate the path model (displayed here in "regression-table" form) of Figure 3.1, now disaggregated by sector. Because we are comparing re-sults across subsamples where the variables have different variances, the results are reported in terms of unstandardized regression coefficients, that is, "*b's*" rather than "betas." The direct effect of academic achievement on predicting job commitment, fear of *proteksia*, and intent to return, which was so central in our path analysis, is very weak for the private sector. Academic achievement has practically no effect on job commitments in the private sector, but it is very powerful for both universities and government. The three sectors differ less with respect to work in the field in Israel, but here, too, the private sector is weakest. Demonstrated academic and professional competence seem to

Table 3.16. *Unstandardized regression coefficients showing opportunity structure and migration intentions for population, disaggregated by sector*

Dependent variable	Independent variables	Private industry	University	Government
A. Job commitment in Israel	Academic achievement	$.004^a$	.142	.188
	Worked in field in Israel	.090	.268	.357
	R^2	.035	.382	.542
B. Fear of *proteksia*	Academic achievement	$-.045^a$	$-.119^a$	$-.254^a$
	Job commitment	$-.117^a$	$-.019^a$	$-.025^a$
	R^2	.011	.044	.140
C. Return to Israel	Job commitment	.501	.780	.784
	Fear of *proteksia*	$-.140^a$	$-.322$	$.110^a$
	Academic achievement	$.025^a$	.119	$.045^a$
	R^2	.033	.380	.279

^{a}The understandardized coefficient is less than twice the standard error.

have little to do with securing a job from a private employer. The opportunity structure within the private sector is highly indeterminate (as measured by R^2, the coefficient of determination), whereas the university and government sectors (particularly the latter) are significantly more determinate (Table 3.16, A).

Given the small sample sizes in the disaggregated sectoral analysis, we find that the relationships with "fear of *proteksia*" are statistically insignificant. However these relationships are consistently in the same direction, that is, fear of *proteksia* is a negative function of academic achievement and professional experience in Israel (Table 3.16, B).

The final effect of these factors on the pattern of expected repatriation is shown in Table 3.16, C. Having a job commitment in Israel encourages students from all three sectors to return home, although the relationship is somewhat weaker in the private sector. The entire process of job acquisition and return is highly indeterminate in the private sector, suggesting that taste, sentiment, chance, or other variables not included in the present analysis may make the difference in that sector. The other two sectors are far more determinate. The one anomaly that appears is that government sector students are *more* likely to return home when they express fear of *proteksia.* However, this finding may well be a function of sampling error; the standard error is twice the size of the coefficient.

The main thrust of the model of the opportunity structure, which we developed earlier, is essentially inoperative in the private sector. Very few private sector students had jobs waiting and few expected to return to Israel. The private sector does not significantly facilitate the repatriation of many students (because its demand for high-level manpower is low) and it does not particularly bring back students of high academic accomplishment.

Summary

In this and the preceding chapter, we have been examining the effects of the education and employment opportunity structures on the movement of students between Israel and the United States. Both opportunity structures rewarded demonstrated competence, and together they acted so as to repatriate the best Israeli students. The consequences of the opportunity structures are particularly striking in light of the fact that they were not constructed to reach this end. The educational opportunity structure, although planned and formalized, was designed without consideration of consequences for migration. The occupational opportunity structure was not "planned" at all; but it becomes visible through the examination of the aggregated acts of the participants in the system.

The combined effect of the two systems can be thought of in terms of joint probabilities. If a student has had a good academic record, the probability of his choosing to enter government service or working in a university is enhanced. In turn, these sectors are particularly hungry for highly qualified manpower and are willing to make long-term job commitments. Thus, the student with a good record will tend to be attracted to those sectors where there is the greatest probability of his record being rewarded by a job offer. The better the match among academic record, sectoral hiring criteria, and sectoral effective demand, the larger the proportion of students who will receive job offers, and the more and the better the students who will expect to return home.

4. Public policy and student migration

We have been treating student migration as a private matter, much like any free market phenomenon. The repatriation of students responded to "invisible-hand" forces that flowed from private interests. As we noted in the first chapter, student migration is a public matter too, on which governments take positions and formulate policies. In this chapter, we shall examine the effects of government activity, both actual and projected.

For the United States, the brain drain is a source of both profit and embarrassment. The nonreturning student represents a gain to the United States of highly skilled manpower. But in terms of American commitment to the development and growth of other nations, the student brain drain represents a loss. Many in American governmental circles feel America's interest lies in the rapid and orderly development of the underdeveloped world. The American foreign aid program and much of America's involvement in international educational exchange are based on this premise.

Such a concern, too, led a committee of the House of Representatives to investigate the brain drain to determine whether American research and development programs, "through their use of scientific manpower from the less developed countries, are in any way colliding with the need for securing the orderly development of those countries."[1] If in fact America's science program, which has been hungry for manpower, has contributed to the brain drain (and, more specifically, student nonreturn), then American policy is operating at cross-purposes, giving with one hand (through foreign aid) and taking away with the other (through the brain drain). Many comments of government officials and of nongovernmental interested parties, such as universities, can be understood in terms of their relative commitment to these two goals of American policy.

Even if America's interests were simple and clear (which is not the case), and America were committed solely to the development of other

69

nations, with no interest in the recruitment of high-level manpower to operate the American scientific and technological enterprise, it still would not be in a position to act unequivocally to stop the brain drain, particularly from less developed countries. Public policy is never written on a *tabula rasa*. With the possible exception of revolutionary situations (which are historically rare), governmental policy initiatives must take into account a preexisting context of moral concerns, bureaucratic structures, and interest groups. To use a statistical metaphor, policy makers have few degrees of freedom in the formulation of new government programs and policies. This problem is not peculiar to the issue of the nonreturning foreign student; it is characteristic of all public policy innovation.

Whether one finds this morally desirable or not, there is an inherently conservative strain in public policy formation, irrespective of the issues involved. Public policy is most effective when it can activate and organize latent self-interest and channel it for the public good. When policy runs counter to the salient and dominant interests and values of those who have a significant stake in the issue, then there is a good chance that policy will be openly flouted or covertly undermined. Paradoxically, then, government intervention is most effective when in a sense it is least necessary, that is, when self-interest and collective interest coincide.[2]

Theoretically, both Israel and the United States could easily stop the brain drain either by not permitting students to study abroad or by forcing those who have studied abroad to return home. Government officials on both sides of the ocean, who are responsible for international educational exchange in all of its ramifications, must be aware of the simple alternatives of either closing borders to keep students from going abroad or using some instrumentality to coerce them to return home. Why, then, don't they simply afford themselves the use of one or more of these instrumentalities?

The explanation lies partly in that both nations view themselves as open societies allowing people to move with maximal freedom in and out of the country. All countries regulate the movement abroad of their nationals through control over the issuance of passports, and the movement of foreign nationals into their country through the issuance of visas. Israel, for its purposes, could withhold passports from students seen as high risks for migration. The United States, by the same token, could restrict visas to those students whose return home seemed reasonably certain. These solutions could create greater problems than those which they might solve. For either country to restrict movement severely would be to violate one of its primary values.

Israel, moreover, has historically defended the right of Jews to return freely to their homeland. During the mandatory period, the Jewish community of Palestine fought the efforts of Great Britain to restrict the flow of immigrants, and Israel has been attempting for years to get the Soviet Union to permit free emigration of its Jewish population. To reverse its policy and restrict migration suddenly would require a radical redefinition of national purpose and ideals. Israel must allow migration, no matter how painful it may be.

Israel faces a second dilemma as a consequence of its educational policy. As was shown in Chapter 2, a significant proportion of its students in the United States went abroad because they could not gain entrance to Israeli institutions. For the individual student with a weaker academic background, the United States has represented a second chance. For Israeli universities (and the government, which supplies most of the operating budget of the universities), the existence of alternatives abroad has reduced the pressure to expand the size (and number) of universities beyond the point deemed desirable. Foreign alternatives serve as a safety valve at home.

Moreover, as we saw in the third chapter, it is the weaker students who contribute disproportionately to the brain drain. Thus, were Israel to introduce a policy of restricting opportunities to study abroad, it would make sense to allow only the best students to go abroad, since they are the most predisposed to return home. By doing so, however, Israel would increase public demand for greater opportunity for higher education at home. This question will be discussed in greater detail in the second half of this chapter.

In the United States, there has been a long struggle to change the American immigration policy which culminated in the nativist revival of the 1920s. The Immigration Act of 1924 set high quotas for the nations of Northwestern Europe, and low quotas for the nations of Eastern and Southern Europe, and for the nonwhite nations of Africa and Asia. Liberal circles understood these immigration acts to be expressions of racism (which indeed they were) and struggled for years to overturn them, finally succeeding by passing the Immigration Act of 1965, in which occupational quotas were substituted for national quotas. To restrict migration now from the less developed nations would mean a return to essentially nativist, racial considerations and would be opposed by the supporters of liberalized immigration policy.

Proposals to enter into bilateral agreements with less developed countries that are losing skilled manpower to the United States have been opposed by authorities who bear responsibility in this area of American policy. In testimony before the Subcommittee on Immigration and Naturalization of the Committee on the Judiciary of the United States Senate, Dr. Charles Frankel, then assistant secretary of state for educational and cultural affairs, expressed the State Department's position on such limitation of migration:

Laudable as the purpose of such an amendment would be, it would in effect restore the concept of country-of-origin to our immigration procedures. It would place skilled individuals from one country at a disadvantage in relation to individuals of the same skills from another country. It would involve the United States in a web of new international arrangements whose net effect was to limit individual choice and initiative. It would place upon us the difficult responsibility of distinguishing between countries in terms of their needs and in terms of whether their efforts at self-development were successful or not.[3]

Eugene V. Rostow, undersecretary of state for political affairs, Department of State, also defended U.S. policy to the same committee:

. . . we should put to one side policies which would further restrict the freedom of the individual to seek his own fulfillment, and his destiny, in the environment he deems most congenial to him. . . . These movements of students and scholars are an indispensable aspect of freedom. In one sense, the universities of the world constitute a single community. . . . Let us avoid any policies which would weaken that tradition, the yeast of the bread of liberty.[4]

Because the United States is the gainer in the brain drain, these statements could be construed as self-serving rhetorical flourish. But State Department officials are not responsible for America's efforts in science and technology, nor are their organizational interests served by the flow of highly qualified manpower into the United States. On the contrary, governments filing complaints about the loss of manpower address them to the State Department, the only part of the American government that is directly exposed to pressures of other governments and which, in turn, represents the interests of other nations in American policy deliberations. However, in the State Department's large policy agenda, concern with the brain drain plays a relatively small role.

Both nationalists and internationalists can be found supporting the free movement of peoples around the world. Nationalists do so because the United States has been the major beneficiary of the migration of high-level manpower. Internationalists are ideologically committed to the notion of a world intellectual community. In trying to assess the relative strength of these factors, one is hard pressed to determine the motives of the supporters of an open-borders policy.

On the organizational level, policy and procedures take into account the fact that several parts of government have an interest in foreign students. The alien who comes to the United States to study becomes involved in a complex institutional and legal network whose purpose it is to facilitate his academic career, supervise his sojourn, and encourage or enforce his repatriation. "A rough count, and probably an oversimplified count, of the Federal departments concerned with international education would suggest that there are about twenty-four or twenty-five, and it may well be that there are forty."[5]

As an alien abroad, the prospective student must deal with the American consular authorities who represent the State Department. As a student, he has an indirect relationship with the U.S. Office of Education, which is responsible to the secretary of health, education and welfare. As an alien in the United States, the student becomes the responsiblity of the Immigration and Naturalization Service of the Department of Justice. In addition to the various governmental agencies that play a role in his career, he is the client of his school, the concern of the Institute of International Education, and the focus of the solicitude of a host of religious, social, and cultural agencies.

Since the Second World War, there have been three major pieces of legislation prescribing the rights and obligations of the foreign student.[6] The most recent codification of the legislation defines a student as:

. . . an alien having a residence in a foreign country which he has no intention of abandoning, who is a bona fide student qualified to pursue a full course of study and who seeks to enter the United States temporarily and solely for the purpose of pursuing such a course of study at an established institution of learning or other recognized place of study in the United States, particularly designated by him and approved by the Attorney General after consultation with the Office of Education of the United States, which institution or place of study shall have agreed to report to the Attorney General the termination of attendance of each nonimmigrant student, and if any such institution of learning or place of study fails to make reports promptly the approval shall be withdrawn. . . .[7]

The law requires the cooperation of the three relevant departments of the executive branch, the school which the student is attending, and the student himself. This last point is made in another section of the code, where it is stated that

every alien shall be presumed to be an immigrant until he establishes to the satisfaction of the consular office, at the time of application for a visa, and the immigration officers, at the time of application for admission, that he is entitled to a nonimmigrant status under section 1101 (a) (15) of this title.[8]

It is, of course, very difficult for the consular office to measure intent. One would expect that those who wish to use the student visa as an illicit form of immigrant visa would be unlikely to indicate their true intent to the consular officer, despite the fact that misrepresentation in application for an American visa carries with it the possible penalty of being *permanently* barred from admission to the United States. However, since it has been relatively simple to obtain a student visa and rather difficult to obtain an immigrant visa from Israel (and other low-quota countries), one would expect that the intent of the statutes would be violated by some would-be immigrants. Only 2 percent of the students overtly expressed the intention to migrate as one of their reasons for coming to the United States as students. However, as was shown in Chapter 3, among those who came to the United States during the period of 1965–6 (i.e., from a few days to one year before filling out the questionnaire), a significant number did not expect to return to Israel, suggesting that student status is consciously used as a route to migration. The law creates the anomalous situation in which its implementation presupposes the cooperation of those whom it is designed to regulate. It also requires the cooperation of the school in a manner inconsistent with the interests and normative commitments of universities, their faculties, and administrators.

The instruments of American policy

There are effectively two points at which the U.S. government exercises some control over the brain drain. The first is in the issuance of visas, and the second is in the adjustment of nonimmigrant status to that of immigrant as a step toward American citizenship. The compromise in principle, which was discussed in the preceding, is expressed in law by the existence of two major visa categories that differ in the relative ease with which persons who hold them may remain in the United States permanently. The history and intent of these visa categories were summarized in 1967 by a former deputy assistant secretary of state for educational and cultural affairs:

Many years ago the State Department, anticipating that under-developed countries might lose their scholars and scientists to the United States, obtained enactment of legislation for an educational "exchange visitor's visa." This visa has been required of all foreign students, scholars, and researchers who visit our country on Government-sponsored or State Department-approved privately sponsored programs. The regulations require that all those who enter with this visa must leave the country at the end of their period of study or research – with certain exceptions granted in cases of extreme hardship or where the national interest has been involved. That this bit of planning and foresight by the Department of State has been effective in limiting the brain drain is attested to by the fact that 99 out of every 100 students and scholars on official U.S. Government programs have left the United States, the vast majority of them to return to their homelands. Strengthening of this legislation in 1961 further enhanced the effectiveness of the exchange visitor visa. Thus, it may be said that Government officials, responsible for U.S. Government and approved privately sponsored exchange programs, have done their part to see that foreign students and scholars go home, trained and with new skills to apply to their own problems. It now remains for the other nations to create political, economic, and social conditions that will inspire those trained and skilled persons to remain in their homelands.[9]

The State Department defense, in effect, argued that when the U.S. government plays a significant role in educational exchange, students return home. Thus, from the State Department's point of view, the United States had done all it legitimately should do to reduce the brain drain. Basing its claim on visa adjustment statistics collected by the Department of Justice, the government argued that "exchange visitors or J visa holders do not appear to be contributing significantly to the Drain. They are required to leave this country for a minimum of two years upon completion of their study here."[10]

By various measures, the government's claim of a low rate of drain among exchange visa holders was correct. Both the State Department data and the data collected for this study show that three times as many F (student)-visa holders had adjusted their status as did J (exchange)-visa holders.[11] Among Israelis, 65 percent of J-visa holders expected to return home, as compared with only 49 percent of the F-visa holders. The first part of the government's claim would appear to be correct. Exchange visitors have been more likely to return home.

What of the implied second claim that they return home because of the law? Is it the statute or is it some extralegal device that brings them home?

Supporting the State Department's understanding of the situation is

Table 4.1. *Perceived difficulty of adjusting visa status by initial visa*

Perceived difficulty of adjusting visa status	Student visa	Exchange visa
Very difficult (%)	5	29
Somewhat difficult (%)	24	29
Not at all difficult (%)	72	42
N (no. in subgroup)	(563)	(76)
Don't know and no answer (N)	532	205

$$\chi^2 = 58.96; \, df = 2; \, p < .001$$

the fact that those who hold exchange visitors' visas are much more likely to feel that it would be difficult to adjust their status to those of permanent resident and, ultimately, U.S. citizen. The responses of our study population, broken down by type of visa held, are summarized in Table 4.1. Their perceptions of the situation are in agreement with the provisions of the law.

That students who hold an exchange visitor's visa are more likely to believe (correctly) that adjusting their status would be difficult, and are more likely to expect to return home, does not necessarily demonstrate that the law is the instrument that repatriates students. The fact that a very high proportion of the students and exchangees (particularly the latter) do not know the legal strictures suggests that the law per se may not be responsible for the apparent effectiveness of the exchange visa provisions. In a classic formulation of the problem, Eugen Ehrlich wrote, "The effect of the state norms for decision is usually very much over-estimated. The whole matter hinges upon action by the parties, who very often fail to act together. Often the statute remains unknown to a considerable part of the population. . . ."[12]

The congruence between law and behavior (which is itself problematic) can occur for reasons that have nothing to do with the law and its sanctions. Often the law codifies the strongly and universally held sentiments of the population that it purports to regulate. At times, the law reflects individual utility and self-interest, so that what appears to be compliance with "state norms" is, in fact, the result of each individual pursuing his own interest in a self-regulating system in which the law contributes little or nothing.[13]

Two sets of questions arise. First, who makes the decision, and by what criteria, to give a student an F or J visa? That is, which students are subject to the rule that forces them to leave the United States after having completed their training? Second, how, in fact, are the rules for adjustment of status actually administered?

If the primary concern is to repatriate as many students as possible, then it would make most sense to give the more restrictive visas to those whose self-motivated return is most questionable. Based on the analysis in the preceding chapter, students with low levels of academic achievement should receive exchange visas if risk is the criterion. The other alternative would be to assign exchange visas to persons whose defection would be most distressing, namely, those in whom their home country had made the greatest investment and for whom there was the greatest need. By the logic of the second alternative, students with high achievement would receive exchange visas.

In most instances, visas are not assigned by the American consul. The consul assigns an exchange visa only when the student is the recipient of an American travel grant. For the others, the consul issues a visa based on the kind of document that the American school has sent to the student. If the student presents a DSP 66 form to the consul, he is issued an exchange visa; if he presents an I-20 form, he receives a student visa.[14] For most students, initial discretion lies with the school. If the student receives documents for one visa and prefers the other, he is free to request the documents he wishes from the school. In the main, schools are willing to accede to his request. Some students prefer the exchange visa because of the tax advantages it offers; others prefer the student visa because of the freedom from the requirement to leave the United States for two years after completing their studies.

Ultimate discretion on visas in most instances, then, resides with the students themselves. Visa categories are not assigned but are elected by the students, in terms of their own perceptions of their needs. The relationships of this choice of visa to other attributes of our study population are delineated in Table 4.2.

In practice, a clear pattern emerges in which exchange visas are held by those with high academic achievement, who have worked in their field in Israel, and who have jobs waiting for them. The net result of this system of allocation is that exchange visas are held by students in whom their home societies have the greatest interest and, precisely because of this interest, these students are more likely to plan to return.

Table 4.2. *Initial visa by academic achievement, work in field, and job commitment in Israel*

	% Received exchange visa	
A. *Academic achievement in Israel*		
(highest degree and grades):		
No degree from Israel	12 (847)[a]	χ^2 = 176.64
Bachelor's		df = 4
Low grades	18 (196)	p < .001
High grades	24 (72)	
Graduate		
Low grades	41 (137)	
High grades	57 (124)	
B. *Work in field in Israel:*		
Did not work in field	7 (688)	χ^2 = 152.65
Worked in field	34 (688)	df = 1
		p < .001
C. *Job commitment in Israel:*		
Does not report job commitment	14 (1135)	χ^2 = 148.89
Reports job commitment	49 (241)	df = 1
		p < .001

[a]In this table and all tables in this chapter, numbers in parentheses are subgroup Ns.

The correlation between visa and intent to return to Israel is spurious, as is shown in Table 4.3. The exchange visa, with its provisions forcing exit from the United States, contributes nothing to repatriation. Insofar as American policy to reduce student brain drain is predicated on the use of the restrictive exchange visa that policy is totally ineffective.[15]

Administering the exchange visitors' program

The role of the Department of Justice

Earlier in this chapter we discussed briefly the complexity built into the administration of the educational exchange acts. There is no specific place in the American government to which the concerned parties can turn with a problem. The "solution" is in many hands, which of course means that no agency of government can be held fully responsible for

Table 4.3. *Correlations of expectation*
to return home by initial visa

Zero-order correlation	.15
Partial correlation controlling for academic achievement, work in Israel, and job commitment in Israel	.01

the shortcomings of the program. Each major government agency that bears some responsibility for the program has many other responsibilities as well. None is evaluated solely or even primarily in terms of its successful administration of its part of the educational exchange program.

The administrative complexity of the program means that individuals (and organizations) who want to circumvent the legal arrangements have a great deal of room in which to maneuver. The gaps between agencies are easily turned into paths of evasion. The lack of a locus of ultimate responsibility makes it simple (and attractive) for each agency involved to "pass the buck." No major interests of any U.S. government agency are served by rigorous enforcement of the various provisions of the educational exchange acts. Once the students are in the United States (having been accepted by a school and having received a visa), the Department of Justice is charged with overseeing them. Of the major governmental agencies involved in the program, the Department of Justice has the smallest natural interest in its effective administration. Largely a domestic agency, it has little concern for America's international relations and none in education per se. Foreign governments with a complaint about the administration of the educational exchange program (e.g., that too many of their students are migrating to the United States) would turn, rather, to the State Department, which, as an international agency, is weak on the domestic front. But the State Department's ability to do anything about the problem is very limited. Those government agencies which might want to administer the program with attention to the wishes of foreign governments have little power to act, whereas those which can act effectively have little reason to do so.

The way in which the law is administered is often as powerful (or at times more powerful) an instrument in influencing or constraining behavior as is the actual text of the statute. The Immigration and Naturalization Service (INS) of the Department of Justice has primary responsibility for the administration of all regulations that apply to aliens in the United States. Matters of visa adjustment, waivers of exchange visa requirements, and similar issues are handled entirely within the administrative courts established by the INS. The INS has a three-tier administrative court structure, parallel to the federal judiciary's primary and appellate jurisdictions. It is very unusual for a case to exhaust the appellate structure of the INS and then to go on to the federal judiciary.

There are two ways in which an exchange visa recipient may seek to adjust his status and seek relief from the two-year foreign residency requirement. He must demonstrate that leaving the United States "would impose exceptional hardship upon the alien's spouse or child (if such a spouse or child is a citizen of the United States or a lawfully resident alien)," or that waiving the requirement would ". . . be in the public interest."[16] Cases based on claims of hardship come directly to the INS, whereas cases involving the national interest are handled initially through the Inter-Agency Board, which is responsible to the Department of State. Effective final decision in cases that come within the purview of INS lies in the hands of the Service; however, the INS operates with the advice (but does not require the consent) of the Department of State. In deciding the case of a plea for waiver of the two-year rule, the position of the INS is that "if an opinion has been solicited from our State Department representatives abroad in the country to which this alien is to return, while it would be a factor to be considered by us in our determination, it would not be a governing factor."[17]

It is not uncommon for the cultural attaché or another foreign service officer serving in the country of the applicant for waiver to oppose the granting of the waiver. It may well be that the country is experiencing a severe shortage of physicians, nurses, or other personnel necessary for the maintenance of the health and welfare of the population of the country of origin. The foreign service officer is probably in a better position to evaluate the extent to which the person requesting the waiver is needed in his country of origin, yet once that person is in the United States, neither the representative of his own country nor the American foreign service officer has any power to block waiver of the two-year residence requirement.

The grounds for granting a waiver by the INS, namely "exceptional hardship" for the applicant's spouse or child, are clearly open to a wide variety of interpretations and permit enormous latitude in the administration of the law. The INS has stated that in the case of exchange visitors, marriage to an American national in and of itself does not qualify the exchange visitor to adjust his status to that of permanent resident, and it has been asserted that "such waivers are not easy to obtain unless exceptional circumstances are shown." However, the INS has taken the position that it must ". . . apply the rule with some liberality, being very anxious to serve the cause of human beings because we are dealing with the impact the return can conceivably have in causing irreparable damage or injury to the lives or professions of these people."[18]

The Department of State has taken a much firmer position on adjustments based on a U.S. governmental agency claim that the applicant for waiver possesses essential skills whose loss would be contrary to the American public interest. The Department of State has pressed for uniform standards among all the government agencies that have established waiver review boards. The difference in attitude toward interpretation of the law is reflected in the fact that 83 percent of the recipients of waivers received them through claims (which were accepted by the INS) of exceptional hardship, whereas only 17 percent were granted on grounds of national interest.[19] It would appear that the INS is oriented toward the needs (and presumably the desires) of the persons involved; the Department of State has been oriented toward maintaining the integrity of the program of educational exchange.

The role of the school in facilitating repatriation

The role of the school begins when, having accepted the foreign student, it certifies to his acceptance by issuing an I-20 or DSP-66 form, which the student then presents to the local U.S. consular official as a document supporting his application for a student visa.[20] The form is an official government document that serves as one of the instruments controlling the entrance of aliens into the United States. Although the school is a nongovernmental agency, it serves as an instrument of control insofar as it certifies to the ability of the candidate to pursue a course of study in the United States and, thus, to enter the United States. Under the law, the college or university has no obligation to encourage the repatriation of the student, nor does it have any legal power to persuade or force him to return home (although it is obliged to report students who violate the terms of their visas). However, the Department of State feels that "the U.S. Government should encourage selected American colleges and universities, with large concentrations of foreign academic visitors from developing countries which are experiencing skilled manpower shortages, to stimulate the return of these visitors."[21]

Is it reasonable to expect colleges and universities actively to encourage the repatriation of foreign students? Both on ideological grounds and in terms of self-interest, the answer has been a resounding no, as is indicated in the following excerpt from a position paper of the American Council on Education:

The American academic institution will best further the legitimate purposes of the foreign scholar and his government, of our own government and of itself, if its relationships to the foreign scholar are professionally and educationally bounded. The institution's first task is to provide the talented foreign individual with the best opportunities it can afford for free intellectual growth. Its primary concern is the development of his talent and skill, not that he is foreign. *In the absence of express commitments that the foreign national will return to his home country, a college or university should be free, in appropriate circumstances, to explore his interest in remaining in the United States.*[22]

The school's lack of interest in repatriating foreign students is expressed both by administration and faculty. Foreign student advisers are client-oriented, working to help the students reach their private goals. The advisers are unconcerned with national goals. In response to the question, "Do you ever discourage students from adjusting status?", one foreign student adviser responded: "Only if we feel that the application will be rejected. We attempt to maintain an excellent working relationship with INS and facilitate their (i.e., the students') dealing with them."

Insofar as faculty become involved, the reports of Israeli students indicate that American professors are more likely to suggest that the best students remain in the United States, just as Israeli professors suggest that they return home (Table 4.4). Because the best students tend to have exchange visas, it follows then that exchange visitors are most likely to be advised to remain in the United States. In our study population, 38 percent of the exchangees reported that their American professors advised them to remain here, as compared with only 25 percent of those who hold student visas. The pattern of advice is particularly strik-

Table 4.4. *American professors' advice by academic achievement in Israel*

Academic achievement in Israel	% American professors advising to remain in the U.S.	
No degree from Israel	24 (847)	χ^2 = 25.66
Bachelor's		df = 4
Low grades	26 (196)	$p < .001$
High grades	37 (72)	
Graduate		
Low grades	37 (137)	
High grades	40 (124)	

ing in the light of the American Council on Education position paper. Exchange visitors do have "express commitments" to return home. However, professors are responsive to the interests of their fields rather than to policy directives of the State Department or the position papers of the American Council on Education.

Israel's policy alternatives

The steps taken by the government of the United States have not been successful because of the nature of the law, the administrative proceedings, and the divergent interests of the several institutions and organizations that deal with foreign students. Barring some change in American policy and/or procedure, the burden of increasing the return flow of students devolves upon the sending countries. Obviously, some measure of nonreturn is inevitable; the concern becomes one of attempting to diminish the flow at the lowest cost rather than adopting measures designed to stop the flow completely.

Any measures taken by the Israeli government and society to decrease nonreturn would have to be consistent with other policies of the society and state. Israel has to find solutions appropriate to the problem, that is the cost of the solution must not be greater than the benefits projected. Israeli policy makers are no freer to translate will directly into policy than are their American counterparts.

In Chapter 3 we noted that the rate of nonreturn is negatively related to the level of education achieved in Israel. This being the case, would it not make sense for Israel to increase the number of university places available, so that fewer of its students would be forced to go abroad for their education and be subject to the blandishments of a far wealthier society? This solution assumes that nonreturn of students is a joint probability; that is, the probability (1) that the student will go abroad and (2) that the student, if abroad, will not return. If the number of students going abroad can be decreased, then the total loss might be decreased (assuming, of course, that an increase in the supply of skills will not create an oversupply of skills that will generate further brain drain). This argument gains support from the fact that, relative to its university population, Israel has a very large number of students in the United States. However, also relative to size, as of 1960, Israel ranked third in the world, following only the United States and the Soviet Union, in the proportion of persons in the relevant age cohort who were in attendance at institutions of higher learning in their native country.[23] Since that period, the number of Israelis matriculated in colleges and universities has increased considerably.

Further, as we noted in Chapter 2, those who come to the United States to study because of the imbalance between supply and demand of university places tend to be the poorer students. Further expansion of the system would perforce mean that additional funds would be invested in persons of lesser value, and the social return on the investment would in all likelihood decrease. As shown in Chapter 2, the 1960s expansion of the university system took place largely in the humanities and related fields. If cost considerations were to play a crucial role in any future expansion, it is clear that expansion would occur in law and the humanities, leading to the situation currently found in many underdeveloped countries where there is an overproduction of unemployed "gentlemen" and an underproduction of the skills necessary to develop the society.

In part, as we indicated in Chapter 2, inability to enter the Israeli university system is a function of early tracking into schools that are not designed to prepare for university training. It may well be that some of those who are tracked out of the academic high school system would do rather well in university if given the proper opportunity. Improving the predictive validity of the matriculation examinations or creating comprehensive high schools might make for a better utilization of the university places that are currently available, but it would not increase the supply of places open to the students. Such a change might also create a more severe bottleneck by increasing the number of students with university ambitions and qualifications.

An appropriate solution would tend to be a "narrow solution." By narrow solution is meant one that would focus directly on the students and which would have minimal implications for the rest of Israeli society. This is taken to be a commonsensical pragmatic guide to public policy formulation generally. There is, of course, another approach that opts for a broad solution, one in which the problem at hand serves as an entering wedge for larger changes in society. The broad approach is concerned not so much with solving the problem presented, as it is with generating more general social change. The broad approach, however, is likely to evoke opposition from those whose own positions or situations are somehow threatened by the change and, thus, will be less successful and/or consume more of the society's resources in attempting to reach the goal.

The considerations we have noted have dealt broadly with the evaluation of the costs of alternative policies. How do we project the probable benefits? In other words, irrespective of social costs, how can we determine whether a policy will significantly increase the rate of repatriation of Israeli students? The benefit side of the cost–benefit equation is composed of two elements: the proportion of the population affected by the policy and the probable impact of the policy on those affected. In the case at hand, more students indicate that they would prefer to return to Israel than actually expect to return. Some students will behave counter to their expressed preferences because some external condition stands between them and their preferred goal. Let us then restrict our discussion to those who strongly *prefer* to return to Israel, irrespective of what they intend to do. Let us assume further that we can identify some of the external conditions which *might* be standing in their way. We then simply take as our first term the proportion of the population indicating that it faces the particular problem. For the second term, we take the difference in propensity to return to Israel between those who do and do not face the problem. Thus, for each possible solution, we can generate a simple measure of policy effectiveness, which is expressed by

$$D_p \ (R_{\bar{p}} - R_p)$$

where D_p represents the distribution of the problem in the population (i.e., the proportion of the population facing the problem); R_p represents the rate of repatriation among those who have the problem, and $R_{\bar{p}}$ the rate of repatriation among those who do not have the problem. The term $(R_{\bar{p}} - R_p)$ is a measure of how great an impact the problem has on the individual level, and D_p how widely diffused the problem is in the population. Thus, if a problem is widely diffused, D_p is large; but if the difference in propensity to return home between those who do and do not face the problem is small, then instituting a policy based on the solution of that problem will yield low aggregate returns. Similarly, if the impact of the problem for those who face it is large but few face it, then the policy will have a low yield. The larger the number generated by multiplying the two terms, the greater the probable benefit of the policy.

This procedure was carried out for a list of problems that Israelis had indicated were of consequence to them. The results are presented in Table 4.5.

Some of the problems on the list lend themselves to narrow solutions, whereas others require significant changes in Israeli society. Both helping students to find appropriate jobs in Israel and relieving them of some of the very high customs duty that is extracted from all Israelis

Table 4.5. *Problems in returning to Israel and measures of effectiveness in the solution of the problems*

Problem	Index of effective- ness
Appropriate job	.075
Housing	.067
Coping with Israeli bureaucracy	.062
Coping with Israeli inefficiency	.035
Financing return transportation	.028
Military reserve commitment	.018
Customs duty	−.021

importing foreign hard goods (e.g., automobiles and washing machines) are narrow solutions. Of the two, it is administratively simpler to relieve the students of customs duty; however, Table 4.5 suggests that this policy would not have any effect. The index generated is actually negative, since it is more likely to be defined as a problem by those who are going to go back without additional encouragement; thus $(R_{\bar{p}} - R_p)$ is negative. Solving the problem may make life pleasanter for those who want to lower customs duty, but it will not bring more Israelis home.

The customs duty solution was, in fact, instituted for a while but was found to be a complete failure. It did not bring home people who would not have returned without additional prodding. It also turned out to generate resentment among Israelis who had not studied abroad. It created a situation in which those who went abroad were rewarded, even though their having studied abroad was often based upon their having failed at home.

Of all the policy areas dealt with, jobs and housing are the most attractive in terms of their probable benefits and their narrowness of scope. The housing problem is a product of the peculiar housing market in Israel. Rental housing is rare, and in order to purchase a house or flat, one must usually be able to put down more than half of the total cost of the housing unit. Thus, if the price of an apartment or house were 200,000 Israeli pounds, the purchaser would have to have 70,000 Israeli pounds in hand at minimum and then assume a mortgage obligation for the balance at an interest rate of approximately 12 to 15 percent, or higher, unlinked to the cost of living, or a somewhat lower rate of interest linked to the cost of living. The problem is not peculiar to the Israeli students in the United States but is faced by all Israelis. A few employers have developed special arrangements for their staff members, whether they have been educated abroad or at home; however, most employers do not have a standing policy for aiding their employees in the solution of the housing problem. If a special program were to be developed to aid the Israelis who have studied abroad, it in effect would discriminate against those Israelis who have continued their studies at home. This would obviously create inequities and resentment, particularly in a society traditionally committed to egalitarian norms. In all likelihood, the housing problem faced by the potential returnee cannot be solved in isolation from the similar problem faced by the Israeli who has studied at home.

The employment situation creates certain problems for the Israeli studying abroad that are not shared by the Israeli studying at home. The Israeli student at home can easily contact potential employers and be interviewed by them on the spot. While still a student, he is in a position to check out the job situation personally and, thus, has considerably more maneuverability than the Israeli abroad, who searches for a job through the mails and through other impersonal contacts. Israeli students in the United States have complained bitterly about the relative indifference shown to them by potential Israeli employers. They have said that their letters are not answered or that when they are answered, the response is often, "Come home and we shall see what is available." A personal approach to a potential employer is by far the most effective way of finding a job; such an approach is less available to the Israeli studying abroad than it is to the Israeli studying at home. The government's role, then, becomes one of facilitating such contact through encouraging (and underwriting) recruitment by Israeli firms among students abroad and through arranging for job-hunting trips to Israel.[24]

Summary

We probably overestimate the extent to which governments can significantly influence the course of events in free and complex societies. By the time a policy initiative moves from the planners to those who are charged with administration and execution, little may be left of the initial impulse. Even where the policy goal remains clear and has been well formulated, the web of interests and of organizational structures is likely to deflect and distort planned social change.

Effective policy operates (or should be operating) with a principle of least effort. Its task in the case at hand has been that of finding the right leverage that would permit Israel to repatriate the largest number of students at the lowest social and economic cost. It attempts to change that which is changeable. American policy, in principle, focused directly on the problem by purporting to force some students to return home. As we have shown, however, in the course of administering the policy, those in government who were most concerned with the problem lost control over execution of policy. Key initiatives were placed in the hands of those who were to be regulated. The schools did not choose to act counter to their own ethos and interests.

The Israeli policy that we have proposed has two major advantages.

First, it seeks its end by rewarding rather than punishing. No one is forced to return home; the policy works *with* the student's wishes, helping to make his private agenda conform to the public need. Second, its administration is simple, requiring only the cooperation of those in whose interest it is to cooperate. No one is called upon to act counter to his interests or values.

5. Some cross-national comparisons

The preceding chapters have been devoted to a close analysis of the effects of two educational systems on critical decisions in the lives of students. We have shown, first, how the differences between the Israeli and American educational systems influenced students' choices about study abroad. Second, we have shown how the articulation of the Israeli educational and economic systems influenced students' thinking about returning home. Having demonstrated the powerful effects of the school system with regard to Israelis in America, we now want to know whether the behavior of Israelis in America is unique, or whether it is characteristic of foreign student populations generally.

In particular, we want to answer the following questions:

Is the flow of students around the world responsive to differences in opportunities for education between the students' home countries and potential receiving countries?

Is the essentially utilitarian model, which we posited to account for Israelis deciding to study abroad, useful and adequate in accounting for the decisions of students from other countries?

What other factors might account for flows of students? Do countries specialize in subject areas, attracting a particular student body? Are the cultural relations created during the colonial period still operative in accounting for particular patterns of bilateral flows?

On the second of the major issues we have raised, namely the question of repatriation of the students, are the basic Israeli patterns characteristic of other national experiences? Is there a worldwide shortage of high-level manpower that moves employers to make job commitments to students going abroad? Do shortages of high-level manpower create an opportunity structure particularly favorable to the academically most qualified students? Do the students, in turn, respond "rationally" to the opportunity structure, leading to the Israeli configuration in which the best students are most likely to return home? Are there variations in national rates of repatriation that can be explained in terms of the students' personal academic histories and their countries' academic systems?

This chapter will deal with two issues: the decision to study abroad and the decision to return home. With respect to both issues, we shall be looking for the effects of the educational system(s) on students' behavior, motives, and intentions. To answer the questions raised, we will analyze two sets of cross-national data. The first data set was collected to replicate and generalize the Israeli study to groups of foreign students in the United States and France. The second set was initially collected to study the behavior of graduate students in the United States without any special thought being given to foreign students per se. However, there were many foreign students in the American graduate student sample and some of the questions asked of them lend themselves to analysis of the issues that have been raised here.

Foreign students in the United States and France

We turn now to the first set of questions and the first cross-national data set.[1] What accounts for particular patterns of flows of students to two of the major host countries, the United States and France? To deal with this and related questions, we have examined data drawn from samples of foreign students in the United States and France. The sample frame specifies students from fourteen less developed countries studying in the United States and France during the period 1971–2. Of these fourteen countries, seven have significant representations in both receiving countries. These are Colombia, Brazil, Chile, Argentina, Iran, U.A.R. (Egypt), and Lebanon. Students from the other sending countries tend to be found almost exclusively either in the United States or France (Table 5.1).

Most of the students in France are nationals of former French colonies or protectorates. Their schools, modeled after the system in metropolitan France, use French as a or, in some instances, the language of instruction. France supplies them with teachers, texts, and materials; their curricula embody French formal standards. The students in the United States come from two major sources. Some are nationals of America's client states (e.g., Korea); others stem from former British colonies (e.g., India), where English is used as the scholarly and scien-

Table 5.1. *Distribution of countries represented by foreign students in France and the United States (full sample; percentages)*

Country	France	United States
Colombia	1	5
Brazil	8	12
Chile	2	2
Argentina	1	3
Senegal	11	0
Ivory Coast	7	0
Cameroun	7	0
Tunisia	34	0
Iran	8	9
U.A.R.	6	2
Lebanon	12	4
Korea (South)	0	10
India	2	45
Thailand	0	9
N (no. in subgroup)	(452)	(785)
	$\chi^2 = 797.63^a$; df = 13; $p < .001$	

[a]The χ^2 is computed on unweighted Ns calculated on weighted percentages.

tific language. Those countries which send students both to the United States and to France tend to have dual cultural traditions.

The clearest case of a dual cultural tradition is Lebanon, in which there are both Anglophone and Francophone schools. Lebanon had been a French protectorate and even before that had been placed under French religious and cultural influence. The French schools (capped by the Jesuit-run Université Saint Joseph) cater in the main to the Maronite Catholics in Lebanon. The American presence in Lebanese education goes back to the founding of the American Protestant missionary school (1825). By 1863 the Syrian Protestant College (renamed the American University of Beirut in 1920) was founded, and it employs English as the language of instruction. Some Lebanese are prepared for higher education in France, others in the United States. Thus, we find Lebanese in significant numbers in France and in the United States.[2]

These differences in national clienteles, which are substantively interesting, raise an important methodological issue. We want to be able to distinguish among sending and receiving countries with respect to the questions posed. Insofar as the two receiving countries do not have comparable distributions of foreign nationals, we cannot be sure that any differences that might appear between the United States and France are really attributable to characteristics of those countries, rather than the sending countries. To get around this problem we have drawn a subsample from the seven shared countries, and will make two sets of comparisons of the French and American foreign student populations. The full sample (N = 14 countries) comparison is useful for describing the overall behavior of students from LDCs in the two receiving countries. The second sample (N = 7 countries) will help isolate the specifically French and American effects.

Field of study and country of study

The American higher educational system is heavily indebted to the European (particularly German) universities. In the process of transforming itself, the American educational system maintained certain peculiarly American notions, among them a utilitarian approach to curriculum and a commitment to educational egalitarianism and flexibility. These notions, visibly present in the nineteenth-century debates over university reform, still retain their central position. They are still among the major factors distinguishing American from Western European higher education. Utilitarianism is expressed concretely in the greater willingness to accept vocational training as a legitimate part of the universities' mandate. As a result, we find a far greater proportion of the foreign students in the United States enrolled in the vocational subjects, namely, engineering and business administration. The study of law is the only clearly vocational area in which the French enrollment exceeds the American (Table 5.2). French legal training is transferable within the Francophone bloc, whereas most American legal training does not prepare the student for non-American legal practices. That the difference between the foreign students in the United States and France is attributable to the receiving countries rather than characteristics of the sending countries is made clear by the seven-country subsample of Table 5.2. If the country of origin is held constant, foreign students in the United

Table 5.2. *Distribution of fields of study represented by foreign students in France and the United States*

Field of study	14-Country sample[a]		7-Country subsample[a]	
	France	United States	France	United States
Agriculture	1	3	2	4
Engineering and architecture	8	39	9	28
Natural sciences and mathematics	38	19	46	15
Humanities, education, and the arts	18	13	13	19
Social sciences	18	10	18	14
Business and public administration	4	15	3	17
Law	12	1	9	3
Health	1	0	0	1
N (no. in subgroup)	(450)	(782)	(184)	(460)
	$\chi^2 = 202.84^b$; df = 7; $p < .001$		$\chi^2 = 110.47^b$; df = 7; $p < .001$	

[a] Percent entries based on weighted Ns; base figures based on unweighted Ns.
[b] The χ^2 are computed on weighted percentages and unweighted Ns.

States are still much more likely to be enrolled in programs in engineering and business.

We alluded earlier to the egalitarianism and flexibility of American higher education (see Chapter 2). Although educational systems generally enroll an ever-decreasing proportion of the relevant age cohort as they move from primary schools to secondary schools into universities, the American educational opportunity structure is far less steeped than most other educational systems with uniform formal criteria for admissions from one stage to the next. The early tracking of students into academic (i.e., university preparatory) and nonacademic schools is characteristic of European school systems and quite uncharacteristic of the American system. The highly decentralized, highly variable American university system is able to afford a place for just about everyone who is prepared to make the effort to find his way. The French educational system (and, to the best of our knowledge, most or all of the other European systems) by contrast is far more centralized, formalized, and far less open. French secondary school students live in terror of the baccalaureate (*bachot*) examinations that control access to the universities of France. Without the *bachot*, a French student has little or no chance of continuing his education.

We found that some Israeli students came to the United States to take advantage of the openness of American higher education. Those students, Second Chancers, were not able to continue their schooling in Israel, largely because of their having been tracked into nonacademic high schools, not having earned a matriculation certificate, or having done poorly on their matriculation examinations. Most of these students were undergraduates. Their coming to the United States was motivated by the push of a relatively closed system and the pull of a relatively open system. The United States offered second chances that were not available at home.

In all, 4 percent of the students in France are classified as Second Chancers, as compared with 14 percent of the foreign students in the United States.[3] In both countries, the Second Chancers tend to be matriculated at lower levels, but the effect of academic status is far greater in the United States than in France (Table 5.3). The Israeli pattern holds for nationals of other sending countries in the United States, but it does *not* hold for the foreign student groups in France.

Table 5.3. *Reason for study abroad by degree candidacy in France and the United States (percent who are Second Chancers)*

Degree candidacy	14-Country sample		7-Country subsample	
	France[a]	United States	France[a]	United States
Bachelor's	5	29	5	31
	(261)[c]	(219)	(86)	(156)
Master's	5	9	5	11
	(109)	(307)	(51)	(160)
Doctorate	2	7	2	6
	(82)	(259)	(47)	(145)
	$\chi^2 = 0.96$[b]	$\chi^2 = 58.87$[b]	$\chi^2 = 0.86$[b]	$\chi^2 = 37.81$[b]
	df = 2	df = 2	df = 2	df = 2
	$p < .6$	$p < .001$	$p < .6$	$p < .001$

[a]The degrees in France are labeled by their American equivalents.
[b]The χ^2 are computed on weighted percentages and unweighted Ns.
[c]In this table and all tables in this chapter, numbers in parentheses are subgroup Ns.

The difference in motives between the foreign students in the United States and France reflects the difference in educational opportunity structure we have described. The American university system welcomes the "casualties" of other educational systems in a way and to an extent that is probably unique in the world.

Academic achievement and returning home

The student brain drain is not a peculiarly American phenomenon. Rather, available data suggest that a significant proportion of foreign students expect to remain in the countries in which they have received their university training. In both the American and French samples we are examining, about a third of the students expected to remain permanently abroad. Later in this chapter, we will examine national variations in migration rates as they reflect characteristics of the students' home country. Here we will attempt to replicate the basic Israeli findings with respect to the relationship among academic achievement, job assurances, and migration.

Almost a third of the students in France and about a fifth of the students in the United States report that they have jobs waiting for them.

Table 5.4. *Job commitment by academic achievement as measured by degree candidacy in France and the United States (percent who report job commitment at home)*

Degree candidacy	14-Country sample		7-Country subsample	
	France[a]	United States	France[a]	United States
Bachelor's	25	9	19	10
	(261)	(219)	(86)	(156)
Master's	36	23	26	47
	(109)	(307)	(51)	(160)
Doctorate	40	28	42	55
	(82)	(259)	(47)	(145)
	$\chi^2 = 8.99^b$	$\chi^2 = 27.59^b$	$\chi^2 = 8.97^b$	$\chi^2 = 75.02^b$
	df = 2	df = 2	df = 2	df = 2
	$p < .01$	$p < .001$	$p < .01$	$p < .001$

[a]The degrees in France are labeled by their American equivalents.
[b]The χ^2 are computed on weighted percentages and unweighted Ns.

Presumably, the same factors motivate employers in their home countries as we suggested were prompting the commitments made by Israeli employers. Facing a shortage of high-level manpower, they were willing to entertain the costs and risks involved in making long-term commitments to those who study abroad. So, too, as among the Israelis, those commitments are made particularly to graduate students (Table 5.4). The full sample of fourteen countries and the seven-country subsample differ somewhat in the distributions and strength of the relationship, but the patterns are the same across the board and are consistent with the Israeli findings. However, the French and American full samples differ with respect to the relationship between academic level and migration (Table 5.5).

In the fourteen-country samples, the higher the educational level of the students in the United States, the more likely are they to expect to return, but for students in France, there is a statistically weak relationship in the other direction. How do we account for this difference? Is it attributable to some quality of the students and their home countries, or to the receiving countries, or to an interaction of sending and receiving countries? A clue to the solution of this problem is presented in the seven-country subsamples.

Table 5.5. *Expectation of returning home by academic achievement as measured by degree candidacy in France and the United States (percent who expect to return home)*

Degree candidacy	14-Country sample		7-Country subsample	
	France[a]	United States	France[a]	United States
Bachelor's	71	60	60	59
	(261)	(219)	(86)	(156)
Master's	69	62	63	67
	(109)	(307)	(51)	(160)
Doctorate	61	76	66	73
	(82)	(259)	(47)	(145)
	$\chi^2 = 2.84^b$	$\chi^2 = 17.72^b$	$\chi^2 = 0.39^b$	$\chi^2 = 6.75^b$
	df = 2	df = 2	df = 2	df = 2
	$p < .3$	$p < .001$	$p < 0.8$	$p < .05$

[a]The degrees in France are labeled by their American equivalents.
[b]The χ^2 are computed on weighted percentages and unweighted Ns.

For students from those countries which are in the seven-country subsample (i.e., not nationals of clear client states), there is no difference between the United States and France in the pattern of relationships. The American fourteen- and seven-country samples do not differ with respect to the pattern of relationships, but there is a difference in the pattern of relationships between the two French samples, which is attributable to the major Francophone countries in the full French sample (i.e., Senegal, Ivory Coast, Cameroun, and Tunisia, which comprise three-fifths of the large French sample). By removing them, the effect of educational achievement on migration tendencies in France and the United States becomes largely the same; namely, the higher the level at which the student is matriculated, the more likely is he to expect to return home (though again, the relationship in France is statistically insignificant).

Although for the foreign students in the United States we could posit a model of pure utilitarian self-interest, this model is not appropriate for the foreign students in France. The distribution of job opportunities among foreign students in France conforms to the instrumental assumptions (as is shown in Table 5.4), but the students' responses to the opportunities (Table 5.5) suggest that other factors, particularly cultural, intervene between the student and his opportunities at home and his repatriation. France has maintained a special relationship with its former colonies. Whereas the relationship of the United States with its clients is largely on the level of government to government (and to some extent is maintained by American-based multinational firms), France has had a large cadre of technical experts and teachers reaching down to the towns and villages in the Francophone bloc. In 1963, of a total of 82,000 technical assistance personnel from developed countries working in LDCs, over 51,000 were from France. Approximately 90 percent of the French personnel were working in Africa (particularly in the Maghreb), and of these, a large proportion were primary and secondary school teachers.[4]

During the colonial period, the best of the students from the French colonies studying in France opted to remain in France. "Since these countries attained independence, the cultural policy and, particularly, the scholarships offered for studies in France contribute to maintain this cultural pull and the prestige of a French education."[5] Just as talent in metropolitan France flows toward Paris, talent in the French Union migrates into metropolitan France. Students whose countries are less "Gallicized" seem to take a more instrumental view of their relationship to France and behave much like their conationals in the United States.

For each of the major issues raised, the responses of the foreign students in the United States were completely consistent with those of the Israelis. A significant proportion of the American sample (particularly undergraduates) was motivated to study abroad by the push of limited educational opportunity at home and the pull of greater opportunity in the United States. When they had jobs waiting for them they were more likely to return home. The greater their educational achievement, the more likely they were to have jobs waiting, and the more likely to expect to return home. The French sample was significantly different with respect to some of these issues, as has been indicated. We now turn to the second of our two samples for further elaboration and development of these themes.

Foreign graduate students in the United States

The second sample was drawn in 1963 and was designed to represent the population of students in American graduate schools. In all, the sample included 20,000 students of whom 3,000, or 15 percent, were foreign students. The subsample of foreign students was further refined to exclude persons who were political refugees (i.e., where we could not assume the free movement between countries), and students from countries where reliable data were not available. These refinements reduced the usable foreign sample to 1,700 students from twenty-one countries.[6]

This sample differs from that analyzed in the first half of the chapter in three significant ways. First, it deals with students in only one receiving country. Second, it is restricted to graduate students. Third, it includes students from countries across a wide range of development. The last point will be useful in examining differences in national *rates* of repatriation.

Personal academic histories and repatriation

We have established in both the Israeli and the first American cross-national sample that better students were more likely to expect to return home: Those who completed their undergraduate work at home and, for the Israeli population, those who had good undergraduate records were most likely to expect to return home. The same pattern emerges in this sample as well. It clearly operates with respect to the question of undergraduate work at home or abroad and is true as well (though weakly so) with respect to the effect of undergraduate grades among those who completed their undergraduate work at home (Table 5.6). Interestingly enough, academic achievement in the United States has little or no effect on the student's plans. It is only that work which is visible to potential employers at home, thus permitting the students to compare themselves directly with the countrymen at home, which seems to make a difference.

We also found in the Israeli case that there was significant variation in rates of repatriation by expected work locus. Israeli students who expected to work in the private sector were less likely to return home. This too seems to be the general pattern, as shown in Table 5.6.

The last parallel for which we have data is the effect of job commitment on repatriation. In the earlier analyses, we took job commitment as an expression of employer need for high-level manpower and as a facilitator of repatriation. Because this sample was not designed specifically to deal with the foreign student population and its problems, there was no direct question on job commitments in the student's home country. However, there is a reasonable proxy available for at least part of the population.

The survey from which these data were extracted was interested primarily in graduate student finances, and it collected detailed information on various forms and sources of stipend support. Among the possible sources listed in the questionnaire was a stipend from a foreign government, which we have interpreted as home country support and sponsorship for foreign students. Among the Israeli students, 80 percent of those who said that they were motivated to study abroad by receiving an Israel government stipend reported jobs waiting for them. Home country support is almost fully equivalent to a job commitment in the Israeli population, and we shall assume the same to be true of this population as well. A significantly higher proportion of students with foreign government stipends expect to return home.

Again we find that the same factors that accounted for Israeli repatriation are significant in accounting for repatriation of students from other countries as well. The basic Israeli findings are confirmed in a graduate student population where one would expect the general effects of education on migration to be attenuated, by virtue of the popu-

Table 5.6. *Expectation of returning home by several measures of academic achievement and employment prospects and plans*

	% Expecting to return home	
Place of Bachelor's		
Home	85 (1397)	χ^2 = 57.87
United States	61 (173)	df = 1
		$p < .001$
Undergraduate grades of those who took Bachelor's at home:		
Above B	86 (1011)	χ^2 = 4.79
B or less	81 (356)	df = 1
		$p < .05$
Prestige of American graduate school attended:		
High	84 (782)	χ^2 = 2.19
Low	81 (918)	df = 1
		$p < .2$
Graduate school grades:		
A, A-	82 (756)	χ^2 = 0.3
B+ or less	83 (931)	df = 1
		$p < .5$
Sector of expected work:		
University	84 (799)	χ^2 = 16.03
Private firm	70 (153)	df = 1
		$p < .001$
Job commitment at home (i.e., received home government stipend):		
Yes	100 (123)	χ^2 = 27.11
No	81 (1577)	df = 1
		$p < .001$

lation's greater homogeneity with respect to educational achievement. Now we turn to a problem and factor(s) for which this sample is particularly well suited, namely the sources of variation in *national rates* of repatriation. In Table 5.7 some of the basic characteristics of the twenty-one countries in the sample are presented for each country.

Table 5.7. *Some educational and development characteristics of the 21 countries represented in the American graduate student sample (total N = 1,700)*

Country	Sample (N)	Rate of secondary school enrollment	GNP per capita	% Bachelor's at home	% attending top 22 American graduate schools	% Own government stipend	% Any stipend
Indonesia	35	4	131	100	18	5	91
Mexico	36	7	262	86	14	4	97
Philippines	86	9	220	93	28	0	66
Iran	30	9	108	78	43	29	88
Colombia	33	11	263	80	17	5	87
Turkey	27	12	220	66	43	4	84
Brazil	22	13	293	98	47	10	69
Thailand	35	15	96	61	45	26	72
India	518	19	73	93	37	1	82
U.A.R.	101	21	142	95	48	40	84
Iraq	24	21	156	82	43	44	86
Israel	39	25	726	71	49	0	51
Chile	25	27	379	100	47	4	100
Korea	83	38	144	71	39	0	84
Canada	302	49	1947	86	55	5	86
New Zealand	20	55	1310	88	56	19	100
Australia	41	65	1316	83	69	2	86
Germany	49	79	927	68	45	8	75
Netherlands	30	87	836	68	49	1	81
Great Britain	94	88	1189	99	56	8	82
Japan	70	98	306	93	63	3	85

Sources: Secondary school enrollment – UNESCO, *World Survey of Education III. Secondary Education* (Paris: UNESCO, 1961); GNP per capita – Bruce M. Russet et al., *World Handbook of Political and Social Indicators* (New Haven: Yale Univ. Press, 1964).

Educational systems and national rates of repatriation

The discussion of student migration on the individual level focused particularly on the relationship between the educational system and the economy, relating both to effective demand. Where there was significant effective demand (as expressed by a job commitment at home), students tended to return home. The student's access to opportunity at home, in turn, was shown to be a function of educational achievement. How is effective demand expressed on the national level and how is it to be measured?

Effective demand on the national level is essentially an aggregated measure of the relationship of supply and demand for high-level manpower in a given country. This relationship (between supply and demand for high-level manpower) can be expressed in a summary figure representing in some way the price of high-level manpower. An appropriate measure is the profitability of investment in education. (The absolute price of labor is *not* the proper measure because it takes into account the general wealth and welfare level of the country.) The greater the demand for educated labor (relative to supply), the higher the rate of return on investment in education. This line of argument assumes that investment in education has at least some of the rationality characteristic of other forms of investment. It also assumes that the market's willingness to reward education is realistic. Given these assumptions, what would we expect to be the relationship between the profitability of investment in education and other characteristics of the country?

In the earlier discussion (Chapter 3), we assumed a relationship between physical capital and human capital. We noted that mandatory Palestine was rich in human capital and poor in physical capital, resulting in a low demand for high-level manpower and in an egalitarian wage structure that was relatively indifferent to educational achievement. With statehood, physical capital increased relative to human capital, creating a greater demand for human capital. The wage structure became less egalitarian and investment in education more profitable.

By moving this perspective from an analysis of the historical relationships of physical and human capital in one country to a cross-sectional analysis across countries, we find an interesting and useful parallel.

Developed countries are rich in both physical and human capital and LDCs are poor in both. This, of course, is roughly what "development" means.[7] Separating out the two kinds of capital, we find that differences in human capital investment are far greater than differences in physical capital investment. Thus, whereas India (as an example), is obviously poor as compared with the United States, it is much poorer in human capital than in physical capital. The United States has 23 times the physical capital and 186 times the human capital (both calculated per worker). India requires both physical and human capital but is particularly short of the latter. In India, investment in education is only 6 percent of investment in physical capital, whereas in the United States it is 44 percent. The more developed the country, the greater the amount of human capital relative to physical capital and thus the lower the *relative* return on investment in education.[8]

Estimates of the profitability of investment in education exist for only a few of the countries in our sample. Because it has been shown that the profitability of investment in education is a negative function of the educational level of the population, we can use school enrollment rates as a proxy for returns on investment in education. We have taken secondary school enrollments as our proxy indicator of profitability of investment in education (and thus effective demand) and of national educational development.[9]

The smaller the proportion of the relevant age cohort attending school in the student's country, the higher the rate of repatriation (Table 5.8). Although American attention has focused largely on the impact of student migration on LDCs, these countries have suffered least from the problem. Because rates of enrollment in school are closely related to other measures of development, including per capita income, it follows that student migration should probably be positively correlated with wealth, which is the case. The higher the per capita income of countries of origin, the more likely are students to remain in the United States ($R = .463$).

The pattern of relationships suggests the steps in the migration decision for foreign students in the United States. Earlier we assumed that Israeli students (and others as well) preferred to live in their own country, among their own people. They decided against returning home when they perceived their opportunities at home to be limited. The first step in the decision, then, is the "push" out of their own country. This decision is based on perceived opportunities at home. After having decided to leave home, they then choose a country of greater opportunity, which exerts a "pull." This decision is based on a comparison

Table 5.8. *National rates of repatriation as a function of educational variables*

Variables	Mean	Standard deviation	Correlation with rate of return home
X_1 (rate of secondary school enrollment in the students' home countries)	35.8	30.7	−.530
X_2 (% students with Bachelor's degree at home)	83.8	12.4	.403
X_3 (% students with government stipend)	10.4	13.3	.345
Y (% expect to return home)	84.0	13.8	—

Standardized regression equation:
$$Y = -.45X_1 + .38X_2 + .25X_3 \qquad (R^2 = .48)$$

among opportunities abroad. Thus, although migration tends to flow from poor to rich areas, rates of migration are higher from the richer areas.

To construct a more complete predictive or causal model accounting for student migration in terms of educational factors, we return to our earlier analyses. We consistently found that completing undergraduate work at home and having a job waiting at home predisposed students to return home. The propensity to complete undergraduate work at home was a function of the supply and demand for places in the universities in the students' home countries. A job commitment at home was a function of an employer's need (unmet by local supply) for high-level manpower. Both these factors and the rates of enrollment in school, then, can be understood in terms of a nation's educational development policy and strategy. For predicting the actual rates of migration we have included the three variables discussed. Each of the three variables has a significant effect on repatriation. Together they account for almost half of the variation in the sample (Table 5.8).

In Table 5.9 we have presented the *observed* estimate of rates of student expectation to return to their home countries and the *expected* rate as calculated by the equation presented in Table 5.8. In the Israeli case, the observed rate of repatriation is 79 percent, and the expected

Table 5.9. *A comparison of observed and expected rates of repatriation for the sample of 21 countries*

Country	(A) Observed value	(B) Predicted value	(C) Standardized residual
Indonesia	100	96	0.4
Mexico	95	89	0.5
Philippines	93	91	0.2
Iran	85	92	−0.6
Colombia	92	86	0.6
Turkey	57	80	−2.1
Brazil	87	95	−0.7
Thailand	100	83	1.6
India	90	89	0.1
U.A.R.	92	100	−0.7
Iraq	97	95	0.2
Israel	79	78	0.1
Chile	98	91	0.6
Korea	76	75	0.1
Canada	74	81	−0.6
New Zealand	95	84	1.0
Australia	77	75	0.2
Germany	62	68	−0.6
Netherlands	65	64	0.1
Great Britain	60	79	−1.8
Japan	90	73	1.5

rate is 78 percent. Although for many Israelis the migration of one person from Israel is a moral scandal and reproach, the equation suggests that the actual rate of migration is just about what it "should" be, given the assumptions of the model, the characteristics of Israeli society, and the Israeli student population in the United States. In Chapter 3 we estimated that the true rate of repatriation for Israeli students was approximately 68 percent. We also found in that chapter that the rate of repatriation for graduate students was somewhat higher than for undergraduates. The observed rate of repatriation of 79 percent found here for graduate students is consistent with the estimate for the total population developed in Chapter 3.

For seventeen of the twenty-one countries, the discrepancy between observed and expected rates of migration is 1 standard error or less (see Table 5.9, col. C). In most instances the factors that have been identified as accounting for individual propensities to migrate do a good job on the aggregate level in accounting for rates of migration. Most countries in the sample approximate the level of migration indicated by predictions based on their educational levels and policies.

Of the four countries that significantly deviate from their expected rate, three are at least plausibly explicable. Japan and Thailand (which have higher rates of repatriation than predicted) have *generally* low levels of migration. That is, few Thais or Japanese of any station in life migrate permanently to other countries. Both Thailand and Japan were politically stable, ethnically and culturally homogeneous countries with strong national identities. They are societies that have been relatively closed to foreigners. Great Britain (which has a significantly higher rate of migration than expected) has had a long tradition of migration, particularly to the states of what was once the empire. Britons find their language spoken around the world. They adjust relatively easily to foreign cultures, in part because many of these cultures are derivatively British. The Turkish discrepancy remains a puzzle.

The three factors (rates of enrollment, place where Bachelor's degree was awarded, job commitment) vary somewhat with respect to the extent to which they are "malleable." Rates of enrollment (and the relationship between investment in human and physical capital and the profitability of investment in education) are least malleable. To change them would require enormous effort and complete control over the mechanism of resource allocation within a country. The proportion of the students taking their Bachelor's abroad is somewhat more malleable. If the Israeli situation is characteristic of other countries, then much of the foreign undergraduate population in the United States comes because of a mismatch of secondary school outputs and university entrance requirements. The better the match between the two school levels, the fewer the students going abroad for their undergraduate work and, presumably, the higher the rate of repatriation. The third factor, job commitment at home, is the most malleable in that it allows more room for individual (i.e., employer) discretion. Here too, however, the individual employer's decision was shown to be a function of characteristics of his sector of the economy.

Insofar as the structural characteristics that underlie the variables accounting for rates of repatriation are fixed, the rank ordering, at least, of repatriation rates should remain fixed. The gross migration rates into the United States are a function of American policy and characteristics as well as of the students' home country characteristics. Changes in the American situation should lead to changes in migration rates. However, it is reasonable to expect that American changes would result in shifting the distribution in toto but should not appreciably change the ordering of the countries.

Summary

By and large, we have found that the same factors that accounted for the movement of students from Israel to the United States accounted for the movement of students from other countries to the United States. The United States plays a unique role in international educational exchange, welcoming both weak and strong students. Weak students are offered a second chance; strong students may study at the furthermost boundaries of their disciplines. The flexibility of American higher education allows for the wide diversity of students and motivating factors. The very different picture in France highlighted this characteristic of American higher education.

In the second half of the chapter, we were able to show how the educational level of his home country significantly affected the student's academic career and his migration plans. The actual rates of intended migration of the twenty-one countries came very close to those which were predicted for them. Most particularly, the Israeli rate of migration shown in this graduate sample falls at about what is to be expected, given the migration rate for Israelis on all academic levels. We have shown in this chapter and those that preceded it that educational systems significantly account for migration propensities, largely through the tie between educational achievement and professional opportunity. In the final chapter, we will turn the problem around and address ourselves to the question of the consequences of education abroad (and the attendant migration) for the countries involved.

6. The social utility of study abroad

We have been attempting to understand two related decisions: why students leave their home countries to continue their schooling abroad, and how they decide whether or not to return home. Both decisions could be understood in the light of the ways in which the educational systems were organized in the countries involved, and of the relationship between the educational systems and the economy. Concrete decisions are made by individuals. As we saw, however, they responded with a high degree of rationality to external social constraints. Where the opportunity structure favored returning home, students planned to return home; where their home country conditions were not favorable, they planned to remain in the United States.

Within countries, favorable conditions were a function of educational achievement, professional experience, and the decision to work in a sector that required highly educated manpower. Across countries, good prospects were a function of the relative scarcity of educated manpower at home. When circumstances allowed a reasonably good life at home, the fact that they would earn more abroad turned out to be a minor factor for most professional workers.[1]

The simple forces that underlie the brain drain have important societal implications. First, within countries, the more education a person has received in his home country, the more likely he is to return home. This is particularly significant in light of the fact that education in most countries is a public investment. The student's share in the cost of his education is for the most part an indirect and small one, incurred largely in the form of forgone earnings.[2] Second, those countries that can least afford to lose any of their investment in education are in fact least likely to lose their students to the United States. The unplanned "social system" of the brain drain is just and compassionate. It responds to two simple rules: (1) you get what you pay for, and (2) you get what you need.

The appearance of the brain drain as a societal problem has come about as a result of the growing belief in the social utility of education. Early theorists suggested that education was economically and socially useful, and their perspective was important in developing the case for educating the masses. It is only recently that education has been introduced explicitly into quantitative analyses of economic and social behavior. Some of the findings simply supply coefficients for what is known by all people: Individuals with better and more education earn more, and countries with educated populations are richer. Other analyses have attempted to tease out the peculiar impact of education itself on national economic development and on individual life chances and productivity.[3] In treating the effects of education on the individual level, one has to eliminate the effect of other factors that are strongly associated with schooling. Thus, the gross variable, number of years of schooling, implies intelligence, motivation, drive, as well as learning. Number of years of schooling is easily measured with reliability. The extent to which that variable actually measures the net effect of education, however, is not completely clear. Similarly, on the national level, although wealth and education are highly associated, the causal order or, for that matter, whether there is any causal relationship at all, is still a matter for debate and discussion. Both wealth and education may be particular expressions of development and of underlying unmeasured (and not directly measurable) variables.[4]

Despite the inability of research to pin down precisely the social effects of education, there is good reason to believe that *some* education has social utility. Technical skills that allow one to build bridges, split atoms, and (less dramatically) engage in sociological analysis are efficiently acquired through formal schooling. General liberal arts education has less in the way of a productive element. The market responds to this difference by paying less to liberal arts B.A.s. By and large, the brain-drain debate has focused on the technical occupations, namely, those occupations for which the connection between schooling and social usefulness is clearest. The U.S. government reports on the problems discussed earlier presented detailed information on the migration of scientists, engineers, and physicians, on the assumption that those occupations were particularly crucial for development. Over and above this consideration is the fact that we can see (or believe we can see) how competence in these occupations is a function of formal education. That link is weaker for many other socially significant occupations, for example, school teachers and entrepreneurs.

There is enough evidence to take seriously the claims made for education as a useful social investment. Assuming no brain drain at all, and assuming the general social utility of education, what is the particular social utility of study abroad? By particular social utility is meant the value to a student's compatriots when he has studied abroad. If all persons in a given country studied abroad, then the social value would be approximately equal to the sum of private values. However, relatively few students study abroad. Of what value is the experience of those few to the many who stayed at home? If all the nations of the world were equally developed and their universities varied little or not at all in quality and curriculum, the question of the social utility of study abroad would be trivial: The effects of a sojourn abroad would be those of travel, not education. The utility of study abroad becomes a significant question only when differences are explicitly taken into account.

The existence of opportunities for education abroad relieves the home country of the need to supply unlimited educational opportunity at home. Israel (and other countries), whose educational system has a series of formal requirements for continuation, can afford to maintain this system where alternatives exist for the casualties of the system. The study abroad option for the excluded students (usually undergraduates) permits the maintenance of the educational status quo at home. It allows governments (and university authorities, whose decisions are significantly influenced by the availability of government funds) to hold down the expansion of higher education. This utility, which we may think of as a latent function of educational exchange, does not directly add to the country's resources. However, it does permit the sending country to save some of its resources for investment elsewhere.

The major rationale for education abroad is its usefulness in redistributing the world's intellectual resources. Formal education is just one instrument for achieving this end. The same purpose may be served by technical advisory teams, business investment, and the sale of technologies (i.e., selling patents).[5] The flow of knowledge follows the same general patterns as the flow of all other goods. The poor countries supply raw materials (i.e., students) from which the rich countries form finished goods (i.e., scientists, scholars, administrators). The rich countries add value (read education) to the primary products that they receive from the poor countries. The intellectual division of labor in the world is such that countries specialize in particular fields and clienteles (see Chapter 5). From one perspective, then, it follows that education abroad is most useful for those countries that cannot offer the required level of education at home. For a developed country, education abroad is no more than an alternative to education at home; for an LDC, education abroad produces something that cannot be produced at home.

Do the countries of the world receive back equally useful and competent scientists, engineers, and professionals? That is, assuming that all students return home, are students from India and Great Britain equally useful to their home countries? The potential contribution of study abroad to LDCs is greater in that the proportional increment to the stock of educated manpower represented by the returning student is far greater. However, for various reasons, one would expect the *quality* of manpower in LDCs to be lower (holding constant the units of schooling completed) – even that manpower which is trained abroad.

The resources available for education in less developed countries are sparse, whereas the requirements for quality education, particularly in laboratory fields on the university level, are considerable. The meager resources are often spread too thinly to supply an adequate education for those few who are fortunate enough to be able to enter universities. The demand on the educational facilities in some LDCs is far greater than the society's ability to supply *quality* education. For example, India's university enrollments grew at the rate of 11 percent per annum, compounded, from 1951 through the late 1960s, resulting in a doubling of enrollments every six and a half years. Inevitably, ". . . curricula are compromised, degree requirements are relaxed, and the standards of the 'pass' are lowered."[6] India's higher education, none too good to begin with, has grown weaker because of excessive growth.

Not only the quantity of resources, but the social and cultural contexts of education in the LDCs have affected the level of technically trained manpower. Traditional Indian education, with its indifference to creative research, was in part displaced, in part supplemented, by the English model of the classic gentleman's education, with its own indifference to scientific research orientation. Prodigious efforts have been made by both governmental and private bodies to develop the institutional framework needed for creative scholarship and science. Yet the results have been extremely disappointing. With few exceptions, independent research has not yet been institutionalized; university positions are few in number, poorly compensated, and particularistic; and political considerations are operative in those institutions which do exist.

One observer commented that Indian scientific organizations,

> . . . governmental or universities, seem to be out of touch with the fresh air of rational discussions by their peers outside the organizations concerned. . . . There is not wide understanding of scientific issues. . . . Science in India as in other spheres of our activities is characterized by widespread bickering and strife, endless discussions most of which are pointless. Scientists appear still to be divorced from national life. This builds up sizable resistance among the lay public against increased expenditures for science in India."[7]

The problems of higher education in India are duplicated in much of the Third World despite individual variations. The Philippines, in which many of the universities are privately owned profit-making enterprises, presents a striking example of a contrasting educational structure leading to a similar result. In this entrepreneurial context, stockholders are interested in a return on their investment, not in high-quality graduates. Inevitably, then, unqualified students are kept on the rolls, university-sponsored research is practically nonexistent, and the general level of competence is low.[8]

Turkish higher education is dominated by a rigid university structure, controlled by a few professors who occupy the major chairs. The government hesitates to intervene in university affairs, leaving policy and administration in the hands of a traditionalist and autocratic old guard. Young innovative faculty are discouraged and the old system, inadequate as it is, is maintained by inertia and self-interest. The net result is that in the main, universities have not been able to attract "scientific and research workers of high theoretical standing and sufficiently numerous to be able to sustain themselves and each other, who can devote themselves to discovering and solving important practical problems and who can also gain confidence of the politically relevant public."[9]

Thus, inadequate resources, traditionalism, and the absence of a research ethic all conspire to make education in LDCs qualitatively inadequate. Less developed countries not only lack adequate numbers of highly trained manpower; the manpower trained at home tends to be of poor quality, working under conditions that do not support and reward scientific and scholarly activity.

Empirical evidence to test the effects of national origin on educational and professional achievement has been drawn from the cross-national sample of foreign graduates in the United States described in Chapter 5. By using the rates of secondary school enrollment among the twenty-one countries as the indicator of national educational development, we have examined the relationship between national level of educational development and personal academic and professional competence.

The first such effect is on the distribution of foreign students among American graduate schools. Using a simple dichotomous classification of American graduate schools into the top twenty-two and all others, we find a significant relationship between levels of development as measured by the rate of secondary school attendance in the students' home countries and the quality (or prestige) of graduate schools.[10] On the individual level, the correlation between these variables is $R = .18$; the aggregate level correlation is $R = .67$. Educational level on the *inter*national level functions much as college quality on the *intra*national level. Students trained in better undergraduate institutions (or more developed countries) enroll in better graduate schools.[11] (Table 6.1,A).

If national level of educational development predicted only the quality of the graduate school in which the student is matriculated, that relationship might be attributed to discrimination on the part of admissions committees. However, we have a second measure of student achievement: their graduate school grade-point averages. Again, it is clear that the level of the student's home country has an effect (though less pronounced) on his graduate school performance, that is, students from LDCs report lower, graduate school, grade-point averages.

The matriculation of students from LDCs in less prestigious graduate schools and their lower level of performance occurs despite the fact that they report somewhat higher undergraduate grades. Generally, undergraduate grades are reasonably good predictors of quality of graduate school attended, and of graduate school grades (Table 6.1, B). However, the undergraduate grades of LDC students are discounted by graduate schools, and undergraduate grades are a weaker predictor of graduate school acceptance and performance for students from LDCs (Table 6.2).

What lingering effects (if any) are there on students' later professional achievements which can be traced back to their countries of origin? For most occupations, direct measurement of professional competence is very difficult. Professionals work in organizations in which their unique contribution to the organization's product or service is not readily seen or measured. One exception to this problem is the research scientist. The major visible work product of scientists is a paper in a learned

Table 6.1. *Two measures of academic success of foreign graduate students in the United States, by national level of educational development and by undergraduate grades in home country*

	% Reporting attendance at one of top 22 graduate schools	% Reporting graduate school grade-point average of A or A-
A. *National level of educational development:*		
High	53 (753)[a]	50 (751)
Low	37 (947)	39 (936)
	$\chi^2 = 43.08$	$\chi^2 = 20.29$
	df = 1	df = 1
	$p < .001$	$p < .001$
B. *Undergraduate grades:*		
Above B	50 (1004)	51 (1004)
B or less	33 (354)	33 (354)
	$\chi^2 = 29.63$	$\chi^2 = 33.18$
	df = 1	df = 1
	$p < .001$	$p < .001$

[a] In this table and all tables in this chapter, numbers in parentheses are subgroup Ns.

journal. Papers vary enormously in quality, so that merely counting papers (i.e., treating each paper as an equally valuable unit) initially strikes one as a terribly gross, undiscriminating measure of work output. Yet it turns out to be a very good measure in the aggregate.[12] Nobel laureates, members of the National Academy, recipients of the Fermi prize - indeed, recipients of any of the major prizes in the natural sciences - have much higher rates of publication than do their less esteemed colleagues.

A small minority of scientists produce the majority of scientific papers. The distribution of paper productivity among scientists who have produced at least one paper has been found to conform to an inverse square law, so that if 100 scientists produce 1 paper each, 25 produce 2 papers each (i.e., $100/2^2$), 11 produce 3 papers each ($100/3^2$), and 6 produce 4 papers each ($100/4^2$), etc. Although predicting the number of papers a scientist will produce from the usual measures of

Table 6.2. *Two measures of academic success of foreign graduate students in United States; each measure jointly by national level of educational development and undergraduate grades in home country*

	Undergraduate grades		
	Above B	B or less	
A. *Prestige of graduate school attended by national level of educational development and undergraduate school grades (% reporting attendance at one of top 22 graduate schools):* National level of educational development			
High	63 (411)	36 (179)	χ^2 = 36.32 df = 1 p < .001
Low	40 (600)	29 (177)	χ^2 = 6.83 df = 1 p < .01
B. *Graduate school performance by national level of educational development and undergraduate school grades (% reporting graduate school grade-point average of A or A-):* National level of educational development			
High	58 (410)	37 (179)	χ^2 = 21.53 df = 1 p < .05
Low	45 (594)	29 (175)	χ^2 = 13.28 df = 1 p < .2

academic and intellectual competence results in weak correlations, one of the few factors found to have any predictive power at all is the quality of the graduate school the scientist attended. Presumably, the predictive power of graduate school quality incorporates both selection criteria and training. Because students from LDCs attend lower quality schools, one would expect them to be less productive scientists. If this in fact is true, is it solely a consequence of graduate school selection (and training) or is there an independent effect of national origin?

To examine these questions, a subsample of doctoral aspirants in physics and chemistry was drawn from the larger cross-national sample of graduate students. Using stringent standards of inclusion, seventy-three individuals met the criteria of having been graduate students in 1963 who expected to earn doctorates in physics or chemistry in American graduate schools. The subsequent productivity of each individual through 1970 was measured by checks through the chemical and physical abstracts and was validated by reference back to the papers in the journals.

The general pattern of productivity conforms roughly to what the inverse square law would predict. Five people produced about half of all the papers, whereas half produced no papers at all (Table 6.3, A). The distribution of productivity by quality of graduate school and by level of educational development of country of origin is precisely that which was predicted (Table 6.3, B). Students from lower quality graduate schools and from less developed countries were less likely to have produced papers. The regression equation (Table 6.3, C) shows that neither background factor is a strong predictor of quantity of papers produced, but of the two, national origin is a better predictor than is the quality of graduate school attended.

Although these data are statistically insignificant (in part because of the small sample size) and limited, they are suggestive. Various observers have commented upon the "gap" between the rich and poor countries of the world and the need to raise the social and economic levels of the poor countries through the infusion of physical capital and technical training. One of the stumbling blocks to significant lessening of the gap is the relatively low capacity of LDCs to absorb and *effectively* exploit capital and training. Obviously, there are individuals of high competence in LDCs, but the overall level of competence appears to be lower than that found in Western Europe, Japan, the United States, and Canada.

Evaluating costs and benefits of the brain drain

America's gain

There is no question but that the United States and other developed countries profit from a "brain gain." American immigration policy in

Table 6.3. *Scientific productivity by national level of educational development and graduate school prestige*

A. *Distribution of papers produced by physicists and chemists in sample:*

No. of scientists producing each number of papers	No. of papers
1	23
1	16
1	14
2	8
1	7
2	5
2	4
6	3
4	2
15	1
38	0

B. *Prestige of graduate school attended and national level of educational development as predictors of producing 1 or more papers:*

	% Producing 1 or more papers	
Prestige of graduate school attended		
Top 22	54 (28)	$\chi^2 = 0.50$
All others	43 (45)	df = 1
		$p < .5$
National level of educational development		
High	56 (39)	$\chi^2 = 2.46$
Low	38 (34)	df = 1
		$p < .1$

C. *Regression:*
Y (number of papers produced)
X_1 (country national educational development score)
X_2 (graduate school quality)
$Y = .166X_1 + .050X_2$ $(R^2 = .028)$

Table 6.4. *Level of education of foreign-trained and of total sample of scientific and engineering workers, by occupation (percentages)*

Level of education (expressed in terms of highest degree earned)	Engineering		Natural sciences	
	Foreign trained	Total sample	Foreign trained	Total sample
Bachelor's	58	78	17	47
Master's	33	19	24	28
Doctorate	9	3	59	26
Unweighted N	(317)	(8,615)	(783)	(13,710)
	$\chi^2 = 82.81^a$; df = 2; $p < .001$		$\chi^2 = 445.51^a$; df = 2; $p < .001$	

[a]The χ^2 is computed on unweighted Ns calculated on weighted percentages.

the post–Second World War years has moved consistently toward easing restrictions on well-educated migrants, irrespective of country of origin, leading to the kinds of flows of manpower briefly noted in Chapter 1. The aggregate figures understate America's brain gain. By using data generated by the 1962 postcensus survey of the American labor force, we are able to present in Table 6.4 a more detailed picture of America's stock of foreign-trained scientists and engineers.[13] For this analysis, a foreign-trained worker is defined as one who has received, at minimum, some post-high-school training outside of the United States.

In all, as of 1962, 3.5 percent of the engineers and 6.1 percent of the scientists in the American labor force were immigrants. Large as these proportions are, in relation to the total foreign-born population in the American labor force, they still understate the contribution of foreign-trained scientists and engineers. As the breakdown in Table 6.4 indicates, the foreign-trained have a much higher level of educational achievement than their American colleagues. Compared with American-trained scientists, foreign-trained scientists and engineers are more than twice as likely to hold doctorates.

In all, 43 percent of the foreign-trained received all of their degrees in the United States; another 21 percent received one or more degrees abroad and one or more degrees in the United States; 36 percent received all their degrees abroad. Thus, up to 64 percent of the sample were foreign students at some point during their training. The 36 percent with foreign doctorates, of course, overwhelmingly earned them in Western Europe. The contribution of the less developed parts of the world is largely in terms of B.A.s and high school graduates.

As we have shown elsewhere, the foreign-trained scientists and engineers are also (1) more likely to be engaged in research; (2) if engaged in research are more likely to be doing basic rather than applied work; (3) express less interest in money and more in working with ideas. The foreign-trained are disproportionately involved in the production of new knowledge and, hence, probably contribute disproportionately to America's scientific and technological preeminence.[14]

The loss of the sending countries

Although it is relatively easy to point to the American brain gain, it is far more difficult to calculate just how much the "drained" countries actually lose through it. In part the problem of loss is made more difficult by the confusion of social utility and social morality. The moral attack on the brain drain comes from a sense of the inequity of poor nations subsidizing rich nations. Why should the United States (or Canada or the United Kingdom) be the beneficiary of the tax-supported education of Indians, Iranians, or Turks? There are two possible answers to this question. One is to reject the assumption that education must be defined as a social investment in future production. If publicly supported education is a gift to the student, then he has a right to do with it what he pleases; if he chooses to migrate, that is his affair. Second, even when education is defined as a social investment, is it really the case that educational policy questions are ultimately decided in terms of social utility and that migration means lost utility?

One cannot infer that what one country gains from migration another country must lose. It is possible that migration may be profitable to the receiving country, while the sending country suffers little or no loss *as a consequence of migration.* Consider the case of medical personnel, where the moral dimension is most visible. A hypothetical physician has decided to migrate from his country where the patient–physician ratio is 3,000:1, the infant mortality rate is 130 per 1,000 live births, and the life expectancy is 40 years. He chooses to live in a country in which the patient–physician ratio is 600:1, the infant mortality rate is 25 per 1,000 live births, and the life expectancy is 70 years. The case may be made that he is deserting an area in which there is a shortage of medical personnel to live in ease and luxury in a country that is well served medically.[15]

Although the instance may be morally compelling, it may also be misleading. Upon closer examination it becomes apparent that the relatively few physicians in the migrant's home country are overwhelmingly located in the capital city, where there is a patient–physician ratio of 500:1. In fact, it turns out that physicians in the capital are grossly underemployed, so that many work outside of medicine in order to earn a living. The government and private agencies have invested little or nothing in medical facilities in the villages, so that effectively there is no professional medical care available outside of the capital. By moral and medical criteria, there is an unmet need for medical care, but in fact the *effective* demand for physicians is low. The migration of underemployed physicians from the hypothetical country to the United States or the United Kingdom occurs without impact on the health care system. The social utility of physicians in the country of origin is low, whereas their utility in the United States is high. When migration occurs as a consequence of oversupply (and underutilization), the waste is improperly attributed to migration.

When, through educational exchange, a country appears to lose some of its "human capital," the extent to which there is a *real* capital value loss depends upon the usefulness of those students if they were to return home. In the case of LDCs, if the flow of students abroad and their return home is not accompanied by change in institutional arrangements, then the actual loss *through migration* would probably be low. Even those students who return home are likely to be relatively unproductive. The brain drain issue cannot be properly discussed and analyzed in isolation from a larger agenda of issues relating educational systems and their social contexts.

Governments subsidize education, increasing the supply of highly trained manpower. They make it relatively painless for an individual to go on in school in that the major expense the student incurs is that of forgone earnings. Where earnings are low without the additional education, then even this indirect expense is low. If the government supports supply and the market demand is low, then of course there will be a manpower surplus that will be underutilized or that will migrate. The mistake governments make is to increase supply through publicly supported education and then allow the marketplace to generate its own demand.

The reason for this irrational strategy is all too clear. The increase in publicly supported higher education is a political response to pressure from an electorate that has come to believe that education is the royal road to prestige, the good life, or simply a way out of the tedium of village life. Because national policy allocating manpower does not match its provision of educational opportunity, the expansion in the supply of manpower often has no parallel in expansion of demand, leading to the unemployment or underemployment of university graduates.

To have experienced a real loss through migration, a country must have had a real need for the lost manpower. In fact, in many instances migration occurs because, at least in the short run, the need (as expressed in effective demand) is not there. The putative loss through brain drain is often generated by the mismatch of the output of the schools and the manpower needs of government, industry, and universities at home. The migration of surplus workers, then, should not really be classified as a brain drain by the losing country, although it may be a brain gain for the country to which they migrate.[16]

The problem for those countries which are actual or potential losers of highly trained manpower is not one of competing with salaries in other countries. Rather, it is one of expressing effective demand by supplying the environment – supporting personnel, colleagues, institutional arrangements, and equipment where necessary – that would permit the potential migrant to use his skills effectively at home. Where that is not done, then effective demand is not present, and migration per se occurs at a low cost. It may well be that the brain drain issue will have been most significant in bringing into focus questions about educational training and development. In the long run, concern about these issues will be more profitable than indemnification schemes predicated on shaky assumptions about manpower loss.[17]

Summary

We can get a reasonably good hold on the problem of the determinants of brain drain. On both the individual and national levels we have been able to show the considerable impact of educational systems on migration decisions and rates. In this chapter we have turned the problem around and have examined some consequences of international educational exchange and the student brain drain.

We found some important differences between LDCs and developed countries with respect to the quality of academic work and later professional output. Students from LDCs attended less prestigious American graduate schools, reported lower grade-point averages, and were less likely to have published a paper. The problem of LDCs, then, is probably not only that of a small number of professionals. Those they have are probably less well trained as well. Calculations of the educational exchange benefits to the sending countries should take into account these differences.

As to the impact of migration, we can *relatively* easily point to the "profits" of the receiving countries. The calculation of losses to the sending countries is complicated by some difficult conceptual problems. Insofar as migration is a consequence of the relative oversupply of manpower, then the problem of the brain drain is really a problem of disequilibrium in supply and demand for high-level manpower. Migration is thus a symptom of a problem rather than the problem itself.

Epilogue

The models developed in this volume have explained student migration and repatriation in terms of relatively simple supply and demand considerations. Study abroad has been described as being in part a quest for a second chance, a consequence of the scarcity of places in Israel (Chapter 2) and other countries (Chapter 5). These patterns are of course time bound: We would expect that as "market conditions" changed, that is, as the supply of places in universities came into better balance with the demand for higher education, the number of persons seeking a second chance through study abroad would decrease.

Recent trends in Israeli student migration

The many changes that have taken place both in Israel and the United States since 1966 and early 1967, when the questionnaire data were collected, may have changed the picture presented here, and might produce different findings if new data were to be collected today. Most important for the study, a balance between educational supply and demand *may* have begun to emerge in some fields in Israel since the early 1970s as a result of critical changes both in demography and the structure of opportunity.

In the 1960s, Israel experienced a demographic "bulge" in the college-age population similar to that in the United States at about the same time. In Israel, the prime years for university attendance are between the ages of 20 and 24, that is, after completion of secondary school and military service. Between 1965 and 1970 the number of Jews in that age category grew from 162,000 to 240,000 – an increase of 48 percent. By 1975, however, there was a projected increase to 250,000 – a growth of only 4 percent. Moreover, it was estimated that this number would even decline to 232,000 by 1980 – a drop of 7 percent for this five-year period. Because part of the "second chance" problem in Israel was generated by the age structure, these population

124

changes would alleviate the pressures on the educational system, decreasing the size of the group seeking a second chance.

At the same time, new institutions were opened and old institutions expanded their capacity enormously, increasing the number of places in Israeli higher education in the 1960s (Chapter 3). By the beginning of the 1970s, the supply of university places had begun to catch up with demand in some fields, making it a bit easier to gain entrance into an Israeli university. Insofar as study in the United States was a response to the scarcity of places in Israel (particularly for undergraduates seeking a second chance), we would expect to find a decline in the annual rate of increase of Israelis studying abroad, and even an absolute decline in Israeli registration in American universities.

This expectation is borne out by the annual census of foreign students, which is published by the Institute for International Education. For 1972–3, it showed 12 percent fewer Israelis registered in American colleges and universities than there had been two years earlier. In 1973, there was a further decrease in the absolute number of Israeli registrations. The visa statistics of the Immigration and Naturalization Service also show a declining rate of annual increase in student visas issued to Israelis in the 1970s as compared with the 1960s.

These statistical series do not necessarily "confirm" our theory. There are problems in the way the data are collected and in making inferences from short time series. It is also possible that in addition to these demographic and institutional factors, college-going tastes are changing in Israel, further complicating the analysis. We can say, however, that the INS and IIE data are consistent with the findings presented in Chapter 2, and with changes in Israeli universities and the age structure during this most recent period.

There also appears to be some attenuation of the class bias in college enrollment that was observed in Chapter 2, although the data indicating this change are somewhat deficient for our purposes. Israel is concerned about the integration and relative success of the "second Israel," namely, persons of Middle Eastern and North African origin. Reflecting that concern, Israeli population tables are routinely presented in terms of ethnic origins. These Oriental Jews, as they are called, are lower in education, occupation, and income as compared with Jews of European origin. By using Oriental origin as a rough proxy for social class, we find some significant changes.

Although the rates of enrollment for Orientals are still low in proportion to the total potential enrollment, and in comparison to the rates of those with Western backgrounds, since 1964–5 the rate of enrollment of students of Oriental origin has been increasing more rapidly than that of Western Jews.

Occupational opportunity and repatriation

An important element in the model used to explain the pattern of repatriation of Israeli students was occupational opportunity in Israel. The best Israeli students, it was seen, were most likely to return home because they were in greater demand. When employment opportunities were disaggregated by sector of expected employment (see Table 3.15), however, it became clear that not all sectors were concerned with high academic achievement. The governmental and university sectors "rewarded" academic achievement with employment, whereas the private sector did not. A change in manpower demands in any of these sectors would be likely to affect both the aggregate rate of repatriation and the type of Israeli who would return.

One of the key factors explaining the demand for highly trained and academically superior students in Israel in the 1960s was the growth of the university system itself, which created not only places to study at home but jobs for Israelis seeking university teaching careers. In the decade between 1959–60 and 1969–70, the number of professors and lecturers in Israeli universities grew from 511 to 3,122 persons – a six-fold increase. Between 1970 and 1972, that number increased at a much smaller rate to 3,748 faculty members. Because the supply of university teachers was provided overwhelmingly by Israelis who had studied abroad, particularly in the United States, and by immigrants, one would expect the decline in rate of growth of higher education in Israel to result in a declining demand for doctorates. Moreover, one would expect that academic achievement would have less "power" in allocating opportunities for Israelis studying in the United States: Academic achievement would remain a powerful factor in allocating opportunities *within* the university sector, but the reduction of that sector as a proportion of total demand would decrease the aggregate demand for Ph.D.s.

In the absence of a new data collection to test such a prediction, one must rely, provisionally, on the recent experience of the Israel Government Bureau for Professionals, which reports a decrease in the demand for the most academically qualified students. As Israeli universities have reduced their demand for faculty, it has become more difficult in recent years for the bureau to find appropriate employment for Israelis who have earned doctorates in the United States.

Israeli government policies may militate against these trends. Recently, the Israeli government has been trying to absorb some of the excess supply of doctorate holders by offering grants to universities, private industry, and other employers for research and development. These research and development units are expected to employ the high-level manpower that would not be employed (and thus might not be repatriated) were free market forces alone permitted to operate. It is still too soon to determine the effect of this program.

The aggregate rate of repatriation is a function of the characteristics and mix of employment sectors and global characteristics of the home and competitor countries. As we showed in Tables 3.15 and 5.6, students expecting to work for universities were more likely to return home than were students who expected to work in the private sector. Because aggregate demand is a weighted average of demand by sector, a decrease in demand for personnel in the university sector would decrease aggregate demand in proportion to the size of the university sector relative to the total population.

In Chapter 5 we developed a model explaining national rates of repatriation that took into account the return on investment in education. It was hypothesized that the lower the rate of return for investment in education, the lower the rate of repatriation. It was further reasoned that the larger the proportion of the population that is educated, the lower the rate of return on investment in education and, hence, the lower the rate of repatriation. We found a significant negative correlation between national level of education and rate of student repatriation.

In predicting the rate of Israeli student migration beyond the middle to late 1960s, it is necessary to take into account the growth of the educational system. As the proportion of the Israeli population with secondary and university education increases, we should expect the effective demand for educated persons to decline, resulting in a decline in the rate of repatriation among Israelis studying in the United States.

Two possible countervailing forces should also be taken into account.

First, if the investment in physical capital has increased apace with the investment in education, then the return on investment in education and, thus, the rate of repatriation may remain stable. Second, we would want to take into account the labor market for high-level manpower in the United States (and other countries attractive to Israelis). Insofar as opportunities have declined in the United States, we should expect a higher rate of repatriation to Israel.

Appendix: population and instrument

The population for this study consisted of all Israelis who had entered the United States to study and who were still present in the United States as of the time of data collection. The following four sources were employed for identifying and tracing the members of the population:

    (1) the address and correspondence files of the Israel Government Bureau for Professionals and the Israel Student Organization in the United States;

    (2) the individual IBM cards for all Israeli students in the United States as collected by the Institute for International Education for their annual foreign student census;

    (3) complete lists of visa recipients maintained jointly by the U.S. Embassy and the U.S. Educational Foundation in Israel, both in Tel Aviv, Israel;

    (4) requests to known members of the population for the names and current locations of possibly missing members of the population not known to us.

The similarity among the three official lists gave us a sense of assurance that we had as complete a list as one could develop. Few names appeared in the supplemental requests made to the students that had not already appeared in one or more of the basic source lists. In all, the sources gave us a bit more than 3,000 persons. Two kinds of persons were eliminated from the population: first, those Israelis who reported that their presence in the United States was the result of their parents having migrated to the United States (see Chapter 2); second, those who could not respond to the Hebrew language questionnaire.

The questionnaire went through several drafts and was pretested on a sample of thirty Israeli students and alumni in the United States. The decision to present the questionnaire in Hebrew was made so as to facilitate completion. As it happened, it also served to help define the population by excluding those who could not read the questions in Hebrew. The thirty members of the pretest sample were all interviewed to determine ambiguities in the questions and their responses. (A copy of the Hebrew questionnaire is available from the author.)

The questionnaire was mailed out to members of the population during the first week in May, 1966. Follow-up mailings continued during the summer and fall of 1966. Responses were analyzed by date of return of the questionnaire and no bias was found as a function of date of response. After eliminating those who were not proper members of the population, there were 1934 completed questionnaires giving a response rate of 67 percent.

Notes

Chapter 1. Introduction: the dimensions of the problem

1 "Anglo-Russian Relations, 1620–4," in *Oxford Slavonic Papers*, ed. S. Konovalov, Vol. IV, as cited in William W. Brickman, "The Development of Education in Tsarist Russia," in *The Changing Soviet School*, eds. George Z. F. Bereday et al. (Boston: Houghton Mifflin, 1960), p. 26.

2 Ibid.

3 Ibid.

4 UNESCO, *Study Abroad*, Vol. 17 (New York-Paris: UNESCO, 1968), pp. 650–3.

5 Brinley Thomas, "'Modern' Migration," in *The Brain Drain*, ed. Walter Adams (New York: Macmillan, 1968), pp. 32–3.

6 The Immigration, Naturalization and Nationality Act (*Public Law* 414) introduced the third preference category for professional and technical workers.

7 U.S., Congress, House, Committee on Government Operations, *The Brain Drain of Scientists, Engineers, and Physicians from the Developing Countries into the United States; Hearings January 23, 1968*, 90th Cong., 2nd sess., 1968, p. 2.

8 Ibid., p. 3.

9 U.S., Congress, House, *The Brain Drain*, 90th Cong., 1st sess., 1967, p. 7. See, too, Herbert G. Grubel and Anthony Scott, "The Cost of U.S. College Exchange Programs." *The Journal of Human Resources* I, 2 (Fall 1966), 81–98. Estimates of financial costs and benefits of brain drain and brain gain can and do vary significantly. For a discussion of the measurement problems, see Chapter 6 of this book.

10 Surveying a wide range of migration literature, Mangalam concludes, "if we exclude the more strictly demographic studies, social problems have dominated the research scene more than any other aspect of migration; consequently nearly half of the publications with more or less theoretical underpinnings are devoted to one social problem or another." J. J. Mangalam, *Human Migration, A Guide to Migration Literature in English, 1955–1962* (Lexington, Ky.: Univ. Kentucky Press, 1968), p. 4.

11 U.S. Congress, House, *The Brain Drain*, 90th Cong., 1st sess., 1967, p. 7 and 90th Cong., 2nd sess., 1968, p. 3.

12 UNESCO, *Study Abroad*, pp. 650–1.

13 Israel's role in educating students from Third World countries is described in Leopold Laufer, *Israel and the Developing Countries: New Approaches to Cooperation* (New York: The Twentieth Century Fund, 1967), Chapter II, pp. 187–200.

14 *Davar*, August 31, 1966.

15 These comments were made in response to the questionnaire distributed to Israeli students.

16 *Ha Tsofeh*, November 17, 1965.

17 Ibid., August 5, 1966.

18 *La Merhav*, October 25, 1966.

19 *Ha Aretz*, December 9, 1966.

20 Claire Selltiz, June R. Christ, Joan Havel, Stuart W. Cook, *Attitudes and Social Relations of Foreign Students in the United States* (Minneapolis, Minn.: Univ. Minnesota Press, 1963), p. ix.

21 Margaret L. Cormack, *An Evaluation of Research on Educational Exchange* (Washington, D.C.: The Bureau of Educational and Cultural Affairs, U.S. Department of State, 1962).

Chapter 2. Coming to America

1 *The Foreign Student: Whom Shall We Welcome?* (New York: Education and World Affairs, 1964).

2 William H. Sewell and Oluf M. Davidsen, *Scandinavian Students on an American Campus* (Minneapolis: Univ. Minnesota Press, 1961), pp. 7-8.

3 Richard D. Lambert and Marvin Bressler, *Indian Students on an American Campus* (Minneapolis: Univ. Minnesota Press, 1956), pp. 29-30. Iraj Valipour, "A Comparison of Returning and Non-Returning Iranian Students in the United States," unpublished Ed.D. thesis, Teachers College, Columbia University, New York, 1961, p. 12.

4 Lambert and Bressler, *Indian Students*, p. 48; Sewell and Davidsen, *Scandinavian Students*, p. 3. At the beginning of the 1960s, 40 percent of the foreign students in the United States were in the natural sciences, whereas in the rest of the Organization for Economic Cooperation and Development (OECD) nations the average figure was only 20 percent [in OECD, *Policy Conference on Economic Growth and Investment in Education, 1962; III: The Challenge of Aid to Newly Developing Countries; IV: The Planning of Education in Relation to Economic Growth; V: International Flows of Students* (Paris: OECD, 1962)].

5 Louis L. McQuitty, "Elementary Linkage Analysis for Isolating Orthogonal and Oblique Types and Typal Relevancies," *Educational and Psychological Measurement* XVII, 2 (Summer, 1957), 207-29.

6 For a description of the graph technique, see J. B. Kruskall, "Multidimensional Scaling by Optimizing Goodness of Fit to a Nonmetric Hypothesis," *Psychometrika* XXIX, 1 (March, 1964), 1-27, "Nonmetric Multidimensional Scaling: A Numerical Method," *Psychometrika* XXIX, 2 (June, 1964), 115-29.

7 For the situation during the 1950s, see H. V. Muhsam et al., *The Supply of Professional Manpower from Israel's Academic System* (Jerusalem: Falk Institute for Economic Research in Israel, March, 1959), pp. v-ix. (In Hebrew with English summary.) The 1963 data are presented in Uri Hurwitz and Malkah Yavneh, "The Development of Manpower in the Scientific and Technological Professions in Israel," mimeographed (Jerusalem: The National Council for Research and Development, 1964), p. 29. (In Hebrew.)

8 "Statistical Bulletin of Israel, Supplements," mimeographed (Jerusalem: The Central Bureau of Statistics, April, 1967), XVIII, 4, p. 120. (In Hebrew.) The rate of matriculation examination passes and the relationship between having passed the matriculation examination and motives for studying in the United States both are based on analysis of the data in the study being reported.

9 The question of the predictive validity of matriculation examinations is discussed in Michael Hen, Rina Doran, and Gad Yatziv, "Do the Matriculation Examinations Predict Success in Institutions of Higher Learning?" *Megamot* XIV, 5 (August, 1966), 359-71. (In Hebrew.)

10 Because of the large number of cells, which makes for both complexity of presentation, and small base figures in some of the cells, the data have been presented in standardized form. Standardization is permitted where interaction of variables does not occur. Standardization is a common procedure in demographic analysis and is beginning to be used in survey analysis as a way of isolating effects of a given variable or set of variables while controlling for one or more variables. For a discussion of the logic of standardization and its

use with survey data, see Morris Rosenberg, "Test Factor Standardization as a Method of Interpretation," *Social Forces* XLI (October, 1962), 53–61.

11 Torsten Husén, "School Structure and the Utilization of Talent," in *Essays in World Education,* ed. George Bereday (New York: Oxford Univ. Press, 1969), pp. 68–92. For comparative data on levels of educational achievement in Israel and other countries, see Torsten Husén, ed., *International Study of Achievement in Education II* (New York: Wiley, 1967), pp. 21–35. An extensive discussion of the relationship between social class and educational opportunity may be found in Diana Crane, "Social Class Origin and Academic Success: The Influence of Two Stratification Systems," *Sociology of Education* XLII, 1 (Winter, 1969), 1–17. For a discussion of the problem in a cross-national perspective, see A. H. Halsey, ed., *Ability and Educational Opportunity* (Paris: OECD, 1961).

12 Report of the Committee for the Development of the Faculty of Mathematics and Natural Science" mimeographed (Jerusalem: The Hebrew University, February, 1965), p. 6. (In Hebrew.)

13 Hurwitz and Yavneh, "Scientific and Technological Professions in Israel," pp. 10–15; Muhsam et al., *Professional Manpower from Israel,* pp. 51–3.

14 On some of the issues in the Israeli medical brain drain, see M. Prywes, "Travel and Emigration of Graduates of the Hebrew University-Hadassah Medical School to the USA," *Harefuah* LXXII, 8 (April 1967), 311. (In Hebrew.)

15 Norman Kaplan, "The Educational Exchange Program: A Pilot Study of Its Impact on Israeli Institutions of Higher Learning," mimeographed (Washington, D.C.: Bureau of Educational and Cultural Affairs, Department of State, December, 1965), especially pp. 26–39.

16 "Report of the Committee on Higher Education," mimeographed (Jerusalem: October, 1965), p. 20. (In Hebrew.) The Israeli government supplies over half of the operating budget of the institutions of higher learning. The extent to which government participation ought to give the government the right to oversee university expansion in terms of government-defined manpower needs has been debated in government and university circles. For some of the basic issues in the argument, see the symposium published in the August 1967 issue of *Hauniversitah,* pp. 46–57. (In Hebrew.)

17 Association of Medical Colleges, "Foreign Students in U.S. Medical Schools," *Datagrams* 5, No. 6 (December, 1963).

Chapter 3. Education and economic opportunity

1 Several indices of subjective satisfaction and commitment to Israel were constructed, and their results examined. Among these were Zionist ideology, salience of Israeli identity, and commitment to friends and family in Israel. Each of the indices was significantly correlated with expectation to return to Israel in a completely self-evident way; however, they were *unrelated* or weakly related to the positions in Israeli social structure that we have examined. Although the introduction of the indices into multiple regression equations would increase the determinacy of the equation, i.e., they would increase the amount of variance "explained," their introduction would make for statistical rather than theoretical explanation and would not serve our theoretical purposes.

2 This is a central and dominant theme in contemporary sociology. For a statement of the problem, with special reference to American society, see Peter Blau and Otis Dudley Duncan, *The American Occupational Structure* (New York: Wiley, 1967), particularly Chapter 5, pp. 153–205.

3 In the original questionnaire, students were given a nine-point ladder scale and they were asked to indicate whether and with what probability they expected to return to Israel. Those who were certain that they would return were weighted 1.0; those who chose the

next position were weighted 0.5; all others were weighted 0.0. These weights approximated the subjective probabilities obtained from the responses of interviewed students. The data were run with different weighting procedures, all of which gave the same *pattern* of results.

4 The IGBP study was initiated solely for administrative purposes. Fortunately, some of the items in the IGBP office form corresponded with questionnaire items, permitting comparisons of the two populations.

5 Goodwin C. Chu, "Student Expatriation, A Function of Relative Social Support," mimeographed (Institute for Communications Research, Stanford University, n.d.).

6 Nadav Halevi and Ruth Klinov-Malul, *The Economic Development of Israel* (New York: Praeger, 1968), p. 72, passim. On the relationship between education and income in Israel at the beginning of the 1960s, see Ruth Klinov-Malul, *The Profitability of Investment in Education in Israel* (Jerusalem: The Maurice Falk Institute for Economic Research in Israel, 1966).

7 Halevi and Klinov-Malul, *Economic Development of Israel*, pp. 34–5.

8 See Fred Sherrow, "The Arabs of Palestine as Seen Through Jewish Eyes," unpublished Master's essay, Columbia University, 1965, Chapter 5. The relative primacy of class struggle and national goals divided Jewish social theorists and activists early on.

9 Joseph Ben-David, "Professions and Social Structure in Israel," *Scripta Hierosolymitana*, Vol. III (Jerusalem: The Magnes Press, 1956), pp. 126–52.

10 Data presented in Yoel Florsheim, *Development of the Jewish Population in Israel, 1948–1964* (Jerusalem: Central Bureau of Statistics, 1967), Special Series, No. 215.

11 A. L. Gaathon, *Economic Productivity in Israel* (New York: Praeger, 1971), p. 50. See, too, A. L. Gaathon, *Capital Stock, Employment and Output in Israel; 1950–1959* (Jerusalem: Bank of Israel Research Department, n.d.), Special Studies, No. 1. For the impact of physical capital investment on the demand for high-level manpower, see Neil W. Chamberlain, "Training Human Capital and the Transfer of Technology to Developing Nations," in *Transfer of Technology to Developing Nations*, eds. Daniel L. Spencer and Alexander Woroniak (New York: Praeger, 1967).

12 A good summary history of Israeli education is presented in *Encyclopaedia Hebraica* (*Ha Entziklopedia Ha Ivrit*), Vol. 6 (Jerusalem and Tel Aviv: Encyclopaedia Publishing Company, 1957), pp. 983–1057. A general overview of Israeli education may be found in U.S., Congress, House, Committee on Education and Labor, *Education in Israel, Report of the Select Subcommittee on Education*, 91st. Cong., 2nd sess., 1970. See, too, Aharon F. Kleinberger, *Society, Schools and Progress in Israel* (New York: Pergamon, 1969).

13 "Statistical Bulletin of Israel, Supplements" XVIII, 4 (April, 1967), 114. This imbalance has been changed more recently.

14 See Chapter 2 of this book.

15 It should be kept in mind that all calculations, rates, and percentages presented refer to the "then resident" population.

16 Those respondents who held an Israeli university degree and did not report their undergraduate grades were distributed randomly between the high- and low-grade categories by degree. Tables and correlations were run with these respondents included and excluded, yielding the same results. The extent to which academic achievement actually contributes to and/or predicts occupational performance is still a debated issue. One study found that American engineers who had high grades received higher starting salaries and continued to earn more, presumably reflecting higher productivity. See Graham C. Kinlan, "Sponsored and Contest Mobility Among College Graduates," *Sociology of Education* 42, no. 4 (Fall, 1969), 350–67. For an opposing perspective, see Ivar Berg, *Education and Jobs: The Great Training Robbery* (New York: Praeger, 1969). Some of the issues and literature are summarized in Donald P. Hoyt, *The Relationship Between College Grades and Adult Achievement* (Iowa City: American College Testing Program, September 1965).

17 Of those who have a job commitment in Israel and have worked in their field in Israel, most are on leave of absence from their jobs.

18 For comparative data on the effects of social class origin on student repatriation, see Iraj Valipour, "A Comparison of Returning and Non-Returning Iranian Students in the United States," unpublished Ed.D. thesis, Teachers College, Columbia University, 1961, p. 32; William H. Sewell and Oluf M. Davidsen, *Scandinavian Students on An American Campus* (Minneapolis: Univ. Minnesota Press, 1961), p. 37.

19 On the more general question of the social location and use of *proteksia* in Israel, see Brenda Danet and Harriet Hartman, "On Proteksia," *Journal of Comparative Administration* 3, no. 4 (February, 1972), 405–34. Also see Brenda Danet, "The Language of Persuasion in Bureaucracy: 'Modern' and 'Traditional' Appeals to the Israel Customs Authorities," *American Sociological Review* 36 (October 1971), 847–59.

20 These findings bring to mind Robert K. Merton's classic paper, "Social Structure and Anomie," published in his *Social Theory and Social Structure*, rev. ed. (Glencoe, Ill.: Free Press, 1957), pp. 131–60. Committed to the end of professional success and lacking the legitimate means to achieve that end, the academically weaker Israeli students opt for an alternative (and deviant) means to reach their end. However, they misperceive the effectiveness of *proteksia* in Israel.

21 The students were asked to indicate what, if any, advice they received about returning to Israel from a set of "significant others" in Israel and the United States. As could be expected, American sources advised remaining in the United States and Israeli sources advised returning to Israel. Our concern here was to find the sources of the advice. In that regard, only the advice of professors and employers could clearly be seen as a response to the academic and professional achievement of the students.

22 When the students were asked to indicate the sector in which they expected to work, they were encouraged to name more than one if they were not sure of their occupational destination. In order to get at the pure effects of each sector, we have restricted the analysis here to those who mentioned only one sector. A separate analysis was performed for all students, i.e., those who mentioned more than one sector, as well as those who were firmly committed to one, and we found the *pattern* of results to be the same as that reported in the following. The major effect of restricting the analysis in the way we have done was to highlight the intersectoral variations.

23 William Consolazio, "Dilemmas of Academic Biology in Europe," *Science* 133 (1961), 1892–6. Consolazio, who was program director for molecular biology at the National Science Foundation, focused particularly on his field.

24 See Victor K. McElheny, "Israel Worries About Its Applied Research," *Science* 147 (1965), 1123–30; and by the same author, "Fundamental Biology at the Weizmann Institute," *Science* 148 (1965), 614–18; Alfred Conrad, "Report on Economic Technology," mimeographed (United Nations Technical Assistance Programme, August 28, 1966).

25 Some of the problems of science and scholarship in Israel and other small countries are dealt with in Joseph Ben-David, "Scientific Behavior in Israel and the United States," *American Behavioral Scientist* VI, 4 (December, 1962), 12–16.

26 Halevi and Klinov-Malul, *Economic Development of Israel*, p. 27.

27 An increasing proportion of Israeli technology has been acquired through purchase abroad rather than creation at home. See Yoram Barzel, "Patents and Economic Activity," mimeographed (University of Washington, Seattle, 1966).

28 Halevi and Klinov-Malul, *Economic Development of Israel*, p. 114.

29 Daniel Shimshoni, "Israeli Scientific Policy." *Minerva* III, 4 (Summer 1965), 441–56.

30 D. Arian, "The First Five Years of the Israel Civil Service," *Scripta Hierosolymitana*, Vol. III (Jerusalem: The Magnes Press, 1956), pp. 304–77. Arian presents an excellent summary of the history and organization of the civil service under the mandate and the early days of

the state. A more recent and more comprehensive analysis of many of the same issues may be found in Donna Robinson, "Patrons and Saints: A Study of the Career Patterns of Higher Civil Servants in Israel," unpublished Ph.D. dissertation, Columbia University, New York, 1970.

31 Arian, "Israel Civil Service," pp. 344–5.
32 Robinson, "Patrons and Saints," pp. 144–6.

Chapter 4. Public policy and student migration

1 U.S., Congress, House, *The Brain Drain*, 90th Cong., 2nd sess., 1968, p. 1.
2 These propositions have been formulated and expressed by both conservative and radical social critics. Their difference resides in their normative conclusions, not in their analyses. See William Graham Sumner, *Folkways* (New York: Dover, 1959), p. 15; see too, Frederick Engels, "Feuerbach and the End of Classical German Philosophy," in Karl Marx and Frederick Engels, *Selected Works*, Vol. II, (Moscow: Foreign Language Publishing House, 1962), p. 493.
3 U.S., Congress, Senate, Committee on the Judiciary, *International Migration of Talent and Skills; Hearings, March 6 and 10, 1967*, 90th Cong., 1st sess., 1968, p. 51.
4 Ibid., p. 4.
5 From remarks of Charles Frankel, assistant secretary of state for educational and cultural affairs, in *The International Migration of Talent and Skills* (IMTS) (Washington, D.C., October, 1966), p. 74.
6 The United States Information and Educational Exchange Act of 1948 (*Public Law 80-402*); Exchange Visitors – Immigration Status, 1956 (*Public Law 84-555*); Mutual Educational and Cultural Exchange Act of 1961 (*Public Law 87-256*).
7 *U.S. Code*, 8, 1101, 15, F.
8 *U.S. Code*, 8, 1184, b.
9 Harold E. Howland, "Brain Drain from the Philippines," *International Educational and Cultural Exchange* (Fall, 1967), pp. 25–6.
10 "The Brain-Drain – Position Taken by the Council on International Education and Cultural Affairs," memorandum dated February 21, 1967, in Council on International Educational and Cultural Affairs, *Some Facts and Figures on the Migration of Talents and Skills* (Washington, D.C.: U.S. Department of State), p. 4.
11 In this chapter we have restricted analysis to those Israelis who entered the United States on one of the two major educational visas, i.e., F (student) or J (exchange), giving a population of $N = 1376$. Most of the others entered initially on tourist visas, which they quickly changed to student visas. For a description of all the visa programs, see Robert M. Klinger, in collaboration with Robert B. Lindsey and Furman A. Bridgers, *Manual of Immigration Regulations and Procedures Affecting Non-Immigrants for Foreign Student Advisers* (Washington, D.C.: National Association for Foreign Student Affairs, 1966).
12 Eugen Ehrlich, *Fundamental Principles of the Sociology of Law*, translated by Walter Moll (Cambridge: Harvard Univ. Press, 1936), p. 368.
13 See, for example, William J. Chambliss, "Types of Deviance and the Effectiveness of Legal Sanctions," *Wisconsin Law Review* (Summer, 1967), 703–19; Johannes Feest, "Compliance with Legal Regulations," *Law and Society Review* 2 (May, 1968), 447–61.
14 These are the two forms most used by colleges and universities in the United States. Information on procedures for allocating visas was supplied by the executive secretary of the American Educational Foundation in Israel.
15 For comparable findings, see Robert G. Myers, *Education and Emigration* (New York: McKay, 1972), pp. 261–5. An attorney specializing in immigration procedures indicated

that an exchange visa recipient having one American dependent has a fifty–fifty chance of adjusting his status, whereas if the exchangee has two American dependents, he can be sure of adjustment of status. An official of the Institute of International Education indicated that a female exchangee married to an American resident or citizen would find no difficulty in adjusting status to that of permanent resident. For a digest of recent cases involving applications for waivers on J-visa recipients, see *Interpreter Releases* 42 (1966). This issue gives one a sense of the way the administrative proceedings actually interpret "exceptional hardships." In September 1961, the Congress noted certain inadequacies in the educational exchange program (see 87th Congress, House Report No. 1094) and worked toward tightening the regulations for J-visa recipients. Analysis of that part of the population which entered the United States after the new law was in effect showed no change in the relationships reported here. It was found that the pattern remained exactly the same as that which has been reported here, irrespective of year of entry into the United States.

16 *Public Law* 87–256, 1961.

17 Mario Noto, associate director of the INS, statement dated 1966, in Council on International Education, *Migration of Talent*, p. 95.

18 Ibid., p. 96.

19 Calculations based on data from Department of State, March 1, 1967, in Council on International Education, *Migration of Talent*, p. 88.

20 In most cases, certification of a school's right to accept foreign students is a rather simple matter: Schools that have been accredited are approved pro forma by the United States Office of Education. There have been instances, however, where approval has been rather problematic and even has been withheld; for example, see United States v. Tod, C.C.A.N.Y. 1924 F. 172. The Tod case decided that a school of business may qualify as an academic institution for purposes of educational exchange. In another case, a school was not permitted to accept foreign students under the provisions of the acts on the grounds that its library facilities were inadequate; see "Matter of Franklin Pierce College: Petition for Approval of School," Interim Decision #1371 in *Administrative Decisions under Immigration and Nationality Laws*, Vol. 10 (Washington, D.C.: Government Printing Office, 1965).

21 Council on International Education, *Migration of Talent*, p. 6.

22 Commission on International Education, "International Migration of Intellectual Talent," *Bulletin on International Education* IV, 10 (November 17, 1966). [Reproduced in U.S., Congress, Senate, Committee on the Judiciary, *Migration of Talent; Hearings March 6 and 10, 1967*, 90th Cong., 1st sess., 1968, p. 145.] Emphasis supplied.

23 Calculations based on figures presented in Angus Maddison, *Foreign Skills and Technical Assistance in Economic Development* (Paris: OECD, 1966), p. 88.

24 Based in part on information supplied by the author, the Israeli government attempted to increase repatriation both by reducing customs duty and facilitating job search. The customs duty solution, as predicted, was completely unsuccessful, whereas the job solution was extremely successful. In facilitating job search, the authorities must beware of creating an artificial market. The government of India had established a national manpower pool that guaranteed a reasonable income to Indian students who had studied abroad while they looked for appropriate jobs in India. The Indian program failed on two counts: first, few Indian students returned as a result of the program; and second, a very large proportion of those who did return had not found employment and continued on the rolls of the manpower pool without engaging in productive work. For a description of the Indian attempt, see S. P. Awasthi, "An Experiment in Voluntary Repatriation of High Level Technical Manpower – The Scientist's Pool," *Economic Weekly* XVII, 38 (Bombay, September 18, 1967). My proposal, then, is not to create a pool but to facilitate specific employment commitments between Israeli employers and students overseas. The extent to which this would be feasible obviously depends on effective demand at home.

Chapter 5. Some cross-national comparisons

1 The analysis in this part of the chapter is based on data collected by Dr. William A. Glaser of the Bureau of Applied Social Research, Columbia University. Dr. Glaser's study ("The Migration and Return of Professionals") is a partial replication and extension of my Israeli study, using several sending and receiving countries. Many of the Israeli questionnaire items were used by Dr. Glaser. I am grateful to him for granting me access to these data.

2 For a description of the Lebanese educational system, see Roderic D. Matthews and Matta Akrawi, *Education in Arab Countries of the Near East* (Washington, D.C.: American Council on Education, 1949), pp. 407–518.

3 In this chapter, a student is classified as a Second Chancer if he checked either of the following as expressing his motivation for study abroad: (1) I was not accepted by a university or equivalent training school in my country of origin; (2) I feared I would not be able to get into a university or training school in my country of origin because of the limited openings.

4 Maddison, *Foreign Skills and Technical Assistance*, p. 21.

5 Michael Bouvier and Marie-France Desbruyères, "France: Immigration of Scientific and Medical Personnel" in Committee on International Migration of Talent, *The International Migration of High Level Manpower* (New York: Praeger, 1970), p. 551.

6 The data for this part of the chapter were initially collected by Seymour Warkov, Bruce Frisbie, and Alan S. Berger, and are described in their *Graduate Student Finances*, National Opinion Research Center, September, 1965.

The respondents were asked "Are you a U.S. citizen?" Those who answered "No, but I expect to stay in the U.S." were classified as intending to migrate. Those who circled the answer "No, and I do not expect to stay in the U.S." were classified as intending to return home. I have shown elsewhere that few foreign students who study in the United States migrate to third countries [Paul Ritterband and Seymour Warkov, "Foreign Trained Scientific and Engineering Workers in the United States: A Comparison with Their American Trained Counterparts," in *Human Mobility*, ed. Robert McGinnis (to be published)].

7 On the relationship between education and other measures of development, see Frederick Harbison and Charles A. Myers, *Education, Manpower and Economic Growth* (New York: McGraw-Hill, 1964), pp. 45–8.

8 For a comprehensive discussion of these issues, see George Psacharopolous, *Returns to Education* (Amsterdam: Elsevier, 1973), pp. 89–97, 101–2, passim.

9 See UNESCO, *World Survey of Education III. Secondary Education* (Paris: UNESCO 1961).

Chapter 6. The social utility of study abroad

1 The ineffectiveness of expected incomes and income differentials as factors in accounting for migration is shown in several studies. See Larry Sjaastad, "The Costs and Returns of Human Migration," *The Journal of Political Economy* LXX, 5, part II (October 1962), pp. 80–93; Myers, *Education and Emigration*, pp. 305–6; W. B. Reddaway, "Wage Flexibility and the Distribution of Labor," *Lloyd's Bank Review* 54 (1959), 32–48, reprinted in B. J. McCormick and E. Owen Smith eds., *The Labor Market* (Middlesex, England: Penguin Books, 1968), pp. 181–99. In this study as well, we find that expected incomes in Israel and the United States are unrelated to migration plans.

2 Psacharopolous, *Returns to Education*, p. 14.

3 The literature on these questions is vast and growing. By and large, economists of education have assumed that the correlation between education and wealth (both on the individual level and the national level) is causal and that education "causes" wealth. This assumption underlies the use of the term "human capital."

4 See for example, Michel E. A. Hervé, "International Migration of Physicians and Students," mimeographed (Washington, D.C.: A.I.D., 1968).

5 On the flow of technology as measured by patent royalty payments, see C. Freeman and A. Young, *The Research and Development Effort in Western Europe, North America and The Soviet Union* (Paris: OECD, 1965).

6 Robert J. Domrese, "The Migration of Talent from India," in Committee on Migration of Talent, *Migration of High Level Manpower*, p. 221.

7 "The National Physical Laboratory," Unsigned, *Science and Culture (India)* XXXI (March 1965), 107.

8 For a description of Philippine education, see Heather Low Ruth, "The Philippines," in Committee on Migration of Talent, *Migration of High Level Manpower*, pp. 46–80.

9 Osman Okyar, "University of Turkey," *Minerva* VI, 2 (Winter, 1968), 213–43.

10 The measure of prestige of American graduate school attended is based on that presented in Bernard Berelson, *Graduate Education in the United States* (New York: McGraw-Hill, 1960), pp. 280–1.

11 For American students in American graduate schools, there is a relationship between quality of undergraduate and graduate institution attended. See John K. Folger, Helen S. Astin, and Alan E. Bayer, *Human Resources and Higher Education* (New York: Russell Sage Foundation, 1970), pp. 188–91.

12 Good summaries of the literature concerning the correlates, determinants, and consequences of scientific productivity are presented in Derek J. deSola Price, *Little Science, Big Science* (New York: Columbia Univ. Press, 1963).

13 These data are reported in full in Ritterband and Warkov, "Foreign Trained Scientific and Engineering Workers." These findings are consistent with data presented in *Scientists and Engineers from Abroad*, NSF 67-3 (Washington, D.C.: National Science Foundation, 1967).

14 Ritterband and Warkov, "Foreign Trained Scientific and Engineering Workers."

15 Our hypothetical physician might come from one of several countries. See, for example, Heather Low Ruth, "The Philippines," pp. 60–70 most particularly.

16 A good summary of the various approaches to the conceptualization and measurement of "human capital" is presented by Anthony Scott, in "The Brain-Drain: Is A Human Capital Approach Justified?" in *Education, Income and Human Capital*, ed. W. Lee Hansen (New York: National Bureau of Economic Research, 1970), pp. 241–90.

17 Further elaboration of these issues may be found in Gary Becker, *Human Capital* (New York: Columbia Univ. Press, 1964); Theodore W. Schultz, *Investment in Human Capital* (New York: Free Press, 1971).

Index